COMMUNICATION EXCELLENCE

Change Your Words,
Change Your World

To Rick -
My Favorite Students

COMMUNICATION EXCELLENCE

Change Your Words,
Change Your World

Brian Polansky, Ph.D.

Arrow Ridge Publishing
Little Rock, Arkansas

For information address:
Arrow Ridge Publishing,
P.O. Box 55144,
Little Rock, AR 72205-5144
info@arrowridgepublishing.com

Polansky, Brian J.
Communication excellence: change your words, change your world /
Brian J. Polansky. – 1ˢᵗ ed.

Includes index.

1. Interpersonal Communication. 2. Interpersonal Relations.
3. Police Training – United States. 4. Persuasion (Rhetoric).

Library of Congress Control Number: 2004118154
ISBN: 0-9763425-6-1

Printed in the United States of America

10 9 8 7 6 5 4 3 2

*This book is dedicated with
admiration and appreciation
to my wife,
Melissa,
to whom I owe everything,*

*to my daughters,
Lauren and Kendall,
who continue to inspire and humble their father,*

*to my mother
who strongly encouraged me
to "write the book",*

*and to all in law enforcement
who serve and protect
the most important people in my life.*

Acknowledgements

Thank you, Arrow Ridge Publishing, for your patience, suggestions, encouragement, persistence, expertise, and amazing attention to the hundreds of details necessary to turn a sixteen-hour seminar into a book: Melissa Street and your staff of professionals.

Thank you for your generous efforts at proofing, editing, and re-editing a very rough manuscript into a publishable manuscript: John G. Street, Cindy Hedrick and Steve Hollowell.

Thank you, Criminal Justice Institute of Arkansas and Don Kidd, for introducing me to the noble community of law enforcement professionals and the professionals who facilitate officer education.

Thank you, Law Enforcement Management Institute, for the opportunity to serve the greatest profession in the great state of Texas.

Thank you for sharing most of life's most important lessons: my professors at the University of Kansas and Stephen F. Austin State University, and my colleagues at the University of Arkansas-Little Rock.

Thank you, Michael, for being both my brother and the one person I have looked up to my entire life.

Thank you to my running group and competitors for all the important ways that you inspire and help me to be the best I can: David, Bill, Steve, Larry, Tom, Hayes, and Brian.

Thank you, Lauren and Kendall, for being perfect in every way!

Contents

INTRODUCTION   1

ONE   You Have Got a Problem   7

TWO   Your Philosophy of Human Interaction   19

THREE   Your Most Important Verbal Skill   39

FOUR   The Art of Conversation   63

FIVE   The Helping Conversation   75

SIX   Errors of Perception   91

SEVEN   Conflict Management   115

EIGHT   Ancient Principles of Persuasion   145

NINE   Why Do People Do What They Do?   159

TEN   Developing Communication Plans   179

ELEVEN   Coping with Chronic Complainers   205

TWELVE   Your Most Valuable Verbal Skill   229

INTRODUCTION

"Hello, I'm a doctor and I'm here to help you!"

Those are always my first words when I present my program of *Communication Excellence* seminars. My seminars have been attended by tens of thousands of folks just like you, people who want to enhance their ability to say just the right thing at the right time. I find most everyone is interested in learning how to effectively use their words to encourage cooperation from others.

Much of my adult life has been spent studying and teaching the topic of effective human interaction. I completed a Ph.D. program in Communication Studies from the University of Kansas, taught as a professor in the Speech Communication Department of an Arkansas university, and today, travel extensively presenting seminars to a wide range of professionals. My seminars are the synthesis of a three-decade effort to identify the philosophies, principles, and strategies of effective human interaction.

I am flattered the seminars receive the highest evaluations possible and proud that participants report the lessons have helped them to say the right words at the right time and avoid saying the wrong thing at the wrong time.

Today, the majority of my work is with law enforcement professionals. I teach in a number of police recruit academies and serve as adjunct faculty to several leadership institutes and schools of law enforcement supervision.

I also work directly with a number of federal and state agencies providing professional development training to police officers. I am especially proud of the feedback I receive from uniformed professionals who report they are finding it much easier to say just the right words in some of the most difficult circumstances.

Last month, I received a note of appreciation from a police detective in La Marque, Texas. He wrote to tell me that a strategy I taught him, in a long ago seminar, was successfully used to recently secure a confession to a local capital murder from a previously uncooperative suspect. Dozens of police agencies have significantly reduced the number of citizen complaints against their officers after their department completed the training. Officers cite case after case where they recently resolved a confrontation with just the right words—confrontations that in the past seemed to require a physical solution.

Law enforcement audiences also report both professional and significant *personal* benefits from attending my seminars. I often hear, "Man, I could have used this stuff two marriages ago!"

WE ALL POLICE BEHAVIOR

I have found that all of us "police" other people's behavior. All of us have roles that require us to verbally encourage cooperation and compliance. My roles of professor and parent have required me to police the behavior of my students and daughters. Management and supervision are "police" roles, as are coach, teacher, and administrator. Unlike the uniformed police officer, most of us have *only* our words to encourage cooperation and compliance. But like the uniformed officer, the better you can use your words, the easier your job will be, and the more success you will enjoy.

My message of Communication Excellence is universal: Improve your words, and improve your world. I have presented to a wide range of students and professionals. Audiences have included police chiefs, teachers, judges, accountants, investigators, engineers, medical professionals, government administrators, and business and sales professionals. All have benefited from taking a hard look at how they are using their words to encourage or hinder their personal and professional success. Over the years, I have seen familiar faces return to my seminars and report that they continue to find value in revisiting the principles of *Communication Excellence* time and time again.

For a number of years, participants asked if I had written a book they could use as a handy reference or to share my message. Until now, the answer had always been, unfortunately, no.

This Book is My Life's Work

I have spent the last three decades observing human interaction, sifting through thousands of years of systematic academic literature, experimenting with strategies, reading textbooks and journals, testing hypotheses, and teaching courses focused on how we can better use our words to ensure our personal and professional success.

If you had done what I have done over the past decades, you would discover there are some universal truths about human interaction. There are some lessons about effective communication that were true thousands of years ago, that are still true today, and will still be true a thousand years from today. Think of this book as a collection of universal truths about human interaction.

Although I teach a number of different seminars with different objectives to a wide variety of audiences, I keep coming back to the same lessons, principles, and universal truths about effective human interaction. The principles you will learn in this book are the same principles I teach in my two-day schools: *Persuasive Skills & Professional Success*, and *Leadership & Communication Excellence*. These are the principles I teach in my professional development seminars with diverse titles, audiences, and objectives:

Communicating with Difficult People,
Team Leadership & Coaching,
Conflict Management & Negotiation,
Communication Excellence for
  Medical Professionals,
Enhancing Client Communication for
  Certified Public Accountants, and
Verbal Fitness for Patrol Officers.

The principles are the same because the principles are universal truths. My seminars and these chapters operate on this assumption: If you do what successful people do, you will be successful!

I Want to be Successful with This Book

If you were to complete a Ph.D. at the University of Kansas in the Department of Communication Studies, you would learn some things about ancient Roman oratory and Greek rhetoricians. You would learn there are some things that were true thousands of years ago about public speaking that are still true today. The first lesson is if you are going to be a successful orator, your success is dependent upon your audience's reaction. Successful orators centuries ago, just as successful speakers today, would get one of three types of reactions from their audiences.

Three Types of Reactions

The first type of reaction was that the audience was particularly impressed with the message and content presented by the orator. The orator's words had such a powerful impact on the audience that they would listen not only with their ears but also with their eyes and their hearts. The message related so directly to their lives that the audience would reach for a recording instrument to create a permanent record of the powerful message and content.

Although I am flattered when I occasionally see participants in my seminars frantically scribbling down notes as I lecture, I never specifically strive for this type of audience reaction.

The second type of reaction successful orators elicited from their audiences was a standing ovation. At the conclusion of these presentations, the audience members didn't exit holding a thick stack of notes recording the message. Instead, the audience was much more impressed with the orator's delivery of the message and how the content was expertly presented. At the conclusion, the audience was compelled to rise to their feet and vigorously applaud the orator because they were so impressed with the speaker and his delivery of the message.

That is nice when it happens, but it is so rare, with my audiences, that I only cautiously hope for that type of success. Rather, I always actively seek the third type of audience reaction whenever I present my message.

The third reaction was one in which the participants were neither eager to record the message nor to stand and cheer the speaker. Instead, at the conclusion, the audience would be compelled to rise to their feet in unison and STAND AND MARCH! Each participant would eagerly march through the door and do exactly what the speaker hoped they would do as a result of his words.

That is the kind of success I hope for with this book. My success is never measured in the hours I present a seminar but rather in the days and weeks after I have spoken. My success with these chapters will, again, only be measured in how much more successful you become at saying just the right words to change your world. I wish us the best of luck!

You will find, within these pages, principles that have helped successful people find the right words to say at the right time. By applying these principles of Communication Excellence, you will have greater success with your words because…after all, I'm a doctor and I'm here to help you!

ONE
You Have Got a Problem

What is your problem?

Some of you have a lot of problems; some of you have just a few problems, but all of you share one common problem. You are a communication professional. Your professional success is dependent upon your ability to use words to get other people to do what you want them to do. Your problem is that you sometimes fail to communicate professionally and appropriately. And for a communication professional, that's a really BIG problem.

As a communication professional, you are under the burden of high expectations. You are expected to always say the right thing to the right people at the right time in the right way. Most of the time you probably do. Sometimes you don't. That is a problem. But don't worry…I'm a doctor and I'm here to help you.

The failure of communication professionals to communicate professionally is a common problem because of high expectations. I stay busy traveling and conducting seminars designed to help reduce the number of times communication professionals fail to meet the high expectations of their audiences.

Recently, I conducted a series of twenty-two *Persuasive Skills* seminars for Texas Police Chiefs. Over the course of two years, every Police Chief in the great state of Texas attended the six-hour seminar. I asked the Chiefs to complete a survey that included:

"What is the biggest complaint you hear from citizens about your officers?" The vast majority of the complaints fit the category: "I didn't like the way I was talked to." In fact, 92% of the Police Chiefs indicated it was their department's Number One Citizen Complaint.

I have heard the same complaint on college campuses, in school classrooms, engineering firms, construction sites, factories, businesses, sales meetings, client conferences, doctors' offices, airplanes, manufacturing plants, airports, restaurants, living rooms, and bedrooms.

The failure to communicate appropriately and professionally, at all times, is a common problem. Saying the wrong thing at the wrong time may also be a problem for you. But don't worry. I am here to help with some new strategies. After reading this book, you will learn the principles and strategies successful people use to succeed with their words.

Nothing New Here

You may be surprised to learn that little of what you will find in these pages is anything you don't already know. Most of these principles you have heard long before picking up this book. Much of this material will confirm what you may have already assumed or discovered about human interaction. Some of the recommended strategies, you may have been intuitively applying for years, and a few of you are going to be delighted to find you have been doing things right all along!

What you have in your hands is a synthesis of thousands of years of systematic study of effective human interaction. You will find, in these pages, a collection of universal truths, principles, and philosophies that were true two thousand years ago and are still true today.

Here is an example of a universal truth (one you already know). *You are going to die.* It is the truth. I am certain of it. Your time is coming to an end, just like mine. None of us has a thousand years to learn the hard lessons, accumulated over the centuries, of saying the wrong thing at the wrong time. But my seminar participants get a day, sometimes two, to take a long, hard look at how they can do a better job with their words by applying some universal principles of communication excellence.

We are all going to die. I believe the greatest legacy we leave behind is not who we were or even what we did but rather what we said. Some of us make a habit of saying the right thing and are building a legacy that will live long after we are gone. I trust most of my seminar participants have had the experience of being the recipient of just the right words at the right time. Most of us would love the opportunity to return the favor to someone else. Well, our time is short, but the opportunities are endless, and the differences our words can and do make are profound.

The Most Important Lesson

I confess. I don't always communicate appropriately and professionally. Occasionally, even with all my education and experience, I manage say just the wrong thing to the wrong person in the wrong way at the wrong time. The people who witness my failures are typically the most important people in my life. I am a husband and a father of two daughters. Some of my greatest failures with words were with the most important people in my life. Some of my biggest regrets in life are what I said at the wrong time and what I didn't say when the time was right.

My Favorite Family Photo

In my seminars, I show a photograph of my wife and two daughters. I love showing the picture because they are absolutely beautiful women, and I am proud to be their husband and father. I use the photo to give proper credit to those who taught me the most important lesson of effective interaction. I learned this lesson not in any classroom or book but from these three women.

When I introduce my family, I am quick to point out that Melissa and I started dating when I was 16 years old. We have been a couple since 1974 and celebrate 30 years of togetherness—24 years as a married couple and now 21 years as parents. Melissa, Lauren, and Kendall have taught me more about effective communication than any of my three degrees, and each has often reminded me of the most important lesson of effective communication: *You don't find a style of communicating that works for you; you have to find a style that works for your audience.*

Living with these three women has taught me this lesson often. Now, back to the photograph. Lauren had recently graduated from high school, and we found ourselves in Cozumel, Mexico. When asked what she wanted for her graduation present, Lauren suggested a trip to learn how to scuba dive. I learned Cozumel is ideal for such a vacation. I booked the trip, charged lessons for all of us to become certified scuba divers, and then charged a bunch of equipment for four novice divers.

Why did I do all of that? Because Lauren pretty much gets whatever she asks for. The reason she gets most anything she asks for is she doesn't ask for much. Lauren has been just an absolute joy since the day she was born, and it doesn't take much to make her happy. She is one of those rare, naturally happy people who are always the most pleasant person in the room.

Teachers absolutely loved having Lauren in their classrooms. Her teachers often described our first child as a teacher's dream— bright, articulate, accommodating, and the rare student who got along with every other student in class. Some of her teachers said she was the best student they had ever taught.

If I asked Lauren to do just about anything, her response was, "Sure Daddy!" Parents could not ask for an easier kid to raise. She seemed to always get up on her own in the morning, feed and dress

herself, and announce when it was time to be taken to school—
sometimes to parents oversleeping in bed.

When I dropped Lauren off at the University of Oklahoma, I
had absolutely no advice for her as she began her new life at the
university. In spite of attending nine years of college, earning three
degrees, and teaching university students for over a decade, I had
no advice for my daughter that she didn't already know and apply.

Her most recent semester, as an OU sophomore pre-med
major, was typical of most semesters of her entire life—Straight A
report card in difficult courses including cell biology, organic
chemistry, and Kiowa (a Native American language practiced by
few). This was NOT a kid we were eager to have fly the nest, and
though we reluctantly dropped her off at a faraway college, we were
confident she would continue to delight her teachers and be both
happy and successful.

When Lauren was young, I tried to interest her in athletic
competition. It never really took. She was much more interested in
more of a cheerleader type role of encouragement. She was an
exceptionally talented ballet dancer and regularly appeared in local
dance productions. She had no use for sports. She had little interest
in proving she was better than anyone at anything. She would
never want to make anyone feel defeated or a loser.

When Lauren was about three years old, we decided we must be
perfect parents because everyone seemed to agree we had a perfect
daughter. We should have another child!

Well, as you may already know, that was the last time we ever
said those words. Not long after Kendall arrived, we realized this
second daughter was quite different from our first daughter, and
Kendall immediately began teaching us a new set of rules about
what is appropriate treatment of this particular audience.

Different Audiences, Different Expectations

My daughters are about as different as two sisters can be. Lauren is blonde and Kendall is a brunette. Lauren is right-handed. Kendall is left-handed. Little sister is taller than big sister. Kendall has long gotten up late and grumpy to a smiling sister eager to greet the day. Lauren typically dressed and fed herself, but Kendall could never find two socks to match without the help of her mother and was dissatisfied with just about any breakfast served. Lauren has trouble spelling and Kendall is a spelling bee champ. Lauren is always the most pleasant person in the room, and Kendall has to be the smartest person in the room. When Lauren is asked to do just about anything, her response is, "Sure!" You ask Kendall to do anything and her response is, "WHY?" Lauren has never competed in anything in her life, but Kendall is eager for competition and is always looking to prove herself better than anybody at anything.

Kendall was one of those little kids born competitive who immediately set out to try and outperform her big sister—eating cereal faster, first one to the car, first to buckle seat belts, first to see a "slug-bug," and first to get out of the car! I would guess that among her first words were "Me first!" To which her big sister would always reply, "But of course, you first!"

Then, when Kendall learned there are actual fields of competition designed to give little girls a chance to defeat other little girls her size, well, from that moment on she was constantly competing in whatever was the sport of the moment.

She was one of those five year-olds who dominate the soccer games by scoring six goals in the first half, and the coach has to put her in as goalie so the score ends up 6-0. Kendall completed a 6.2-mile race when she was a kindergartner and a triathlon the next year. She won the city swim championships in the backstroke and butterfly every year she competed as an elementary student. She scored 30 points in a basketball game when she was ten years old, the same year she completed her black belt in Tae Kwan Do. She is now a high school student in the state's largest school district. As a 15 year-old freshman, she was on the varsity team roster and contributed to an undefeated season that culminated with a victory in the girls state championship soccer game.

She also recently outscored her entire family on her first attempt at a college entrance exam.

Cooperative Vs. Competitive Audiences

Lauren is quick to ask for help and open to suggestions. Kendall prefers to figure out things alone and is quick with an answer.

I don't get to talk to Kendall the way I get to talk to Lauren. I sure better not talk to Lauren the way I sometimes have to talk to Kendall. Sometimes, both of them either don't like what I said or how I said it. And then Melissa has yet another set of expectations about what is an appropriate way for me to talk to her and our daughters. I am reminded *you have to adapt to your audience.*

This applies whether you are speaking to an audience of 1001 or an audience of one. If you fail to adapt to the different but important audiences in your life, then you will probably have problems in important areas of your life.

If You Want to Change Your World, You Have to Change Your Words.

Your Image

Your image is almost wholly dependent on how you choose to interact with the most important audiences in your life—the people you live and work with.

Most of the adjectives people use to describe other people, if not physical attributes, are based on their communication style. Imagine these possible descriptions of your colleagues at your new job: "Bob is the loud, crude, and obnoxious one over there. He is talking to Rhonda who is kind of quiet and shy, but do not get her started on her cats. Next to her is Jim. Jim is a selfish, egocentric braggart who thinks he is so important. He is talking to Janet. Janet is also vain and is hung up on herself as well, but he is a jerk, and she's just self-centered, and you can't trust either of them with a secret. This office is home to our village idiot, and in that one is our complaining malcontent, and in the back corner is Anne, the religious nut. Here is Mr. Sarcastic, and there is the Queen of the Inappropriately Angry Response. Everyone here thinks I am just a regular guy, and I am sure you will fit right in somewhere."

If you want to improve your image, you have got to improve your words.

Your Relationships

You have met the most important people in my life. Now, let us take a moment to consider the people in your life. Pause and reflect on the most important people in your life.

Now then, each of your important relationships is either better or worse than it was a month ago. Each relationship is better or worse because of how you chose to talk to the most important people in your life.

If you want to improve your relationships, you have got to improve your words.

Your Stress

I often appear in front of very stressed audiences: first responders to crime scenes, police working late shifts, professionals dealing daily with stressed-out victims and offenders. I don't have to remind them they do not get paid very well for what they are asked to do—serve an exceptionally stressful role in society and protect an often thankless community at a job which requires a second job and a working spouse just to pay the bills. I can only imagine the kind of stress that comes from working in the protection of others.

A lot of us are in deeper debt this month when compared to last month in spite of our second jobs. That kind of stress, I can imagine. I have been broke. I went to college for nine years and paid or borrowed my way to three degrees. I know, all too well, what it feels like to go deeper and deeper into debt, month after month. Here is another universal truth: ***Money problems cause a lot of verbal problems.***

Ever Work for an Idiot?

I ask my audiences if they have ever had the distinct privilege of working directly for a complete idiot. You may be surprised how often I get a nearly unanimous affirmative response.

I have worked for some idiots in my many jobs, and that is stressful. Your mind races constantly with the complete lunacy of some idiot placed in a position of authority and decision-making. Each day that you work for an idiot is worse than the day before, and that is stressful!

Ever Have an Idiot Work for You?

If you have ever been in management or supervision, you know the stress of having your performance judged on the performance of a team of idiots. Sometimes, you may have a team of competent employees with the exception of one or two idiots on the team. Policies and procedures are pretty straightforward and most people get it—just do your job. But sometimes, as supervisor, you are stuck with an idiot who seems to consistently say or do something only an idiot could say or do. That is a lot of stress for a supervisor.

That Really is a Lot of Stress!

Financial stress, work stress, scheduling stress, sleep deprivation, stressful co-workers, and stressful jobs—that is a lot of stress faced daily by many. Sometimes, in an effort to get away from the stress of work, we retreat to the sanctuary of our own home only to be met at the front door by even more people who seem dedicated to adding even more stress to our already unbearably stressful lives.

Under stress, you may lose control of your words and say something regrettable to someone important. Then, as a justification, you may proclaim, "WELL EXCUSE ME…BUT I AM UNDER A LOT OF STRESS RIGHT NOW!"

To that, I say no kidding. Of course you lose control of your words when you are under a lot of stress. It is easy to communicate professionally and appropriately when the environment is stress-free and your audience absolutely adores you. But communication professionals communicate professionally no matter how stressful the situation and no matter how their audience talks to them. I believe the biggest favor I do for my audiences is to give them a reminder. I remind each participant that after today:

You can no longer blame other people
for what comes out of your mouth!

For some folks, this has been a real handy excuse for a long time. Those folks have had a ready explanation as to why they said something less than appropriate or professional: "Why did I say that? Well, it is her fault because of what she said first." Unfortunately, that excuse is no longer valid at the end of the day for my seminar participants. Taking that excuse away is the biggest favor I can do for any participant. Most of us already know:

When we take absolute responsibility for our words,
we become absolutely more responsible with our words.

What Do You Want?

What do you want more than anything else? How do you define success? If you are like me, the one thing you want most is to be happy. I know that if I am successful, then I am happy. Happiness and success just seem to go together. I also know my success is dependent on my ability to use my words to get people to do what I want them to do. And, just like you, the more successful I am with my words…the happier I am.

There you go…Chapter One is a review of the introductory comments I make at the beginning of my *Communication Excellence* seminars. Included were a number of the universal truths we will revisit often in subsequent chapters. Chapter Two is where we roll up our sleeves and get to work on the job of finding the right words to say at the right time to ensure our success.

Chapter One Review:
You Have Got a Problem

You are a communication professional who sometimes
  fails to communicate professionally.

"I didn't like the way I was talked to" is a common complaint.

You have to find a verbal style that works for your audience.

Do what successful people do, and you will get similar results.

Your success depends on your words.

Life is short and you are going to die.

Your legacy will not be who you were or what you did;
  your legacy will be what you said.

Improve your image by improving your words.

Improve your relationships by improving your words.

Control your stress by controlling your words.

You can no longer blame other people for what you say.

When you take absolute responsibility for your words,
  you become absolutely more responsible with your words.

Improve your words and improve your world.

Your success and your happiness are dependent on your
  ability to say just the right thing at the right time.

TWO
Your Philosophy of Human Interaction

Take out a blank piece of paper (I suggest using the blank space to your left), put a pen in your hand, and do me this favor. Please fill the blank page by writing down your personal philosophy of human interaction. A philosophy is a set of principles that guide your interaction with others.

I give my audiences 60 seconds to list the principles that guide them in their efforts to say the right words at the right time. Take as much time as you would like, but start now...GO!

TIMES UP!

At the conclusion of 60 seconds, I say, "Set your pens down and look at what the people sitting beside you wrote down." Some see a still blank page in their neighbor's hand. Some participants stopped writing at just two or three words, some after just one full sentence. Others seem to have lots of advice they can share on the topic.

Often, I see others write, "I talk to people the way they talk to me." Once, I asked a tough looking veteran police officer what he had written down. He responded, "I TALK TO THEM IDIOTS EXACTLY THE WAY THEY TALK TO ME!"

His answer led me to ask him and his colleagues a question. I asked, "How many of you, in your professional duties, occasionally have to talk to an idiot?"

Predictably, everyone in the room raised their hand or nodded in agreement. Then I asked, "If you are talking to an idiot and are guided by the Principle of Verbal Reciprocity: *I talk to people the way they talk to me*, what do you sound like to the rest of us?"

That is the Idiot's Philosophy of Human Interaction, and it is surprising how often we fall victim to the problem of talking to people the way they talk to us! The Principle of Reciprocity is more of an observation of human nature than a philosophy. Sure enough, most folks have a tendency to talk as they are being talked to! However, a philosophy must rise above human nature.

The Most Popular Principle

If there is one principle I see written most often as a major component of my participants' philosophy of human interaction, it is some version of "The Golden Rule." If there are only three words I see on a participant's once blank page, those three words are usually The Golden Rule. Some can produce the full biblical verse:

MATTHEW 7:12 *So in everything,* **do unto others what you would have them do unto you,** *for this sums up the Law and the Prophets.*

I am delighted to see this principle written down. The Golden Rule is one thing we can just about all agree on. Essentially all religions have a version of The Golden Rule, as do most codes of law and justice. Democracy is built on this principle. Below are versions of The Golden Rule from a number of religions:

HINDU: This is the sum of duty; do naught unto others which if done to thee would cause thee pain.

CONFUCIANISM: Do not do unto others what you would not have them do unto you.

ISLAMIC: No one of you is a believer until he desires for his brother that which he desires for himself.

BUDDISM: Hurt not others in ways that you would find hurtful.

JEWISH: Whatever thou hatest thyself, that do not to another.

SIKH: As thou deemest thyself, so deem others.

PROBLEMS IN APPLICATION

Still yet another version of the above principles that I often see on my participants' once blank page is "I treat people the way I expect to be treated."

There are two words in the principle—*I treat people the way I expect to be treated*—that are often the source of a number of problems. Those two words that can create a lot of problems are obvious to most participants: I EXPECT.

Using your expectations to guide your interactions can create problems. Some people have exceptionally high expectations of what is an appropriate way for them to be addressed. They have lots of rigorous rules about propriety and social convention. Other people have few rules about human interaction—feel free to talk to them however you wish, call them any name in the book, treat them with less than complete respect, and that is just fine. They have very low expectations about human interaction.

Your expectations probably fall someplace in the middle of the two extremes. When you are guided by only your own expectations, you are going to violate the expectations of about half of your audiences. That is a problem for you.

To help my participants with a principle that avoids the problem of expectations and takes advantage of the Principle of Reciprocity, I suggest the Platinum Rule of Human Interaction.

THE PLATINUM RULE

*Treat people better than they expect, and
you can expect to be treated better.*

If there is one principle that would immediately improve your Philosophy of Human Interaction, one you could embrace as you march out the door to change your world with your words, I believe it is The Platinum Rule. This principle sums up my research into the laws, rules, and principles of human interaction: *In all things, treat people better than they expect!*

A LITTLE MORE HELP

For those who have difficulty expressing their personal philosophy of human interaction, I offer some more assistance. I recognize I have had the advantage of specifically studying the topic since 1976. I also recognize I have the advantage of decades of personal research into thousands of years of systematic academic and philosophical reflection of many others before me on the topic of effective interaction with words. With that experience, I can help fill that blank page with the principles that make up an appropriate and effective philosophy of human interaction.

I have found there are a handful of principles that consistently float to the surface, across the centuries, across cultures, across relationships, personal and professional, which guide us in our efforts to say just the right thing. In essentially every seminar I present, I share four principles.

FOUR UNIVERSAL PRINCIPLES

Everyone wants to be important.
No one wants to look stupid.
Everyone wants to be appreciated.
Never criticize, condemn, or complain.

PRINCIPLE ONE:
EVERYONE WANTS TO BE IMPORTANT

Another popular choice I see written is, "Treat people with respect." I am delighted to see that because it reflects this first principle. It is "important people" who both deserve and expect our respect. VIPs get treated with the utmost respect because they are seen as particularly important people.

I ask my participants to now take a good look into the eyes of the person seated to their left and their right. I call attention to those seated on the front row and ask everyone to take a good look at them. I then ask everyone to turn around and take a good look at those seated comfortably on the back row.

After we all get a good look at everyone in the room, I point out something they all have in common. I remind them they are in a room full of people who want to be important. To everyone's left and right are people who feel it's important to do important things.

Occasionally, I point out another thing they have in common: They don't get paid very well. I often have audiences of police officers, firefighters, schoolteachers, and military professionals. I believe one of the reasons society doesn't richly compensate those in these professions is that there are so many people who will practically volunteer for the opportunity to make important differences in the lives of others.

I remind them they are seated in a room full of people who want to be important. I then remind those participants of something about everyone else *not* in that room that day. They are just like you: They want to be an important person. They want to be treated with value, dignity, and respect!

I do not know which God you pray to. I trust my God sees all of us on the good earth as a child of God. As a father, I assume The Father expects His children to be treated with value, dignity, and respect, just like this father. Now, if one of my participants marches through life violating His expectations, I fear they may have bigger problems than I can help them with.

As we have seen, every culture has some version of The Golden Rule as a founding tenet of their culture and civilization. The principle is neither uniquely Western nor Christian. Sometimes, the language is to treat others as you hope your mother would be treated; sometimes it is your brother; still others, your father, but the principle is universal. You know you expect to be treated as if you were someone important. Therefore, it is clear: ***Treat others as if they were an important person.***

Principle Two: No One Wants to Look Stupid

All of us are human. None of us are perfect. All of us occasionally drop the ball and look or say something stupid. It is inevitable.

It is in those moments that we probably recognize Principle Two: No one wants to look stupid!

If we make the mistake of doing something stupid, there is usually someone in our audience who is absolutely delighted to point out our stupidity to others. Some people seem to exist for the sole purpose of pointing out our occasional stupidity.

Do you know someone like that? Do you know someone who loves pointing out your occasional stupidity? The one person in my life who gets the biggest kick out of pointing out my stupidity is my 16 year-old daughter. Imagine that! And I know why.

You may know someone like Kendall, competitive to the point of always having to be the smartest person in the room. My young daughter is so bright she has figured out she doesn't have to prove she is the smartest person in the room. All she has to do is prove that she is in a room full of idiots and she wins by default!

So, I have to remind my young daughter of what my oldest daughter seems to know intuitively—pointing out how stupid people are is just about the stupidest thing you can do! And here is why. When you have stupid people getting away with their stupidity, do they ever admit it? Most don't. So, you are once again in another stupid argument, arguing with a stupid person over the stupid thing he or she said or did.

No one wants to look stupid. To prove it, I do this with my seminar participants. I ask them to take one more look around at each of the other people in the room. Then I ask, "Which one of you is the stupidest person in the room?"

Predictably, no one in the room raises their hand. Sometimes, they point to a colleague in the room as a candidate, but typically no one raises their hand. I use the response to, once again, point out no one in here wants to look stupid, just like no one out there!

IT HAS GOT TO BE ME

Occasionally, seminars do not always go as planned. When I spoke to my first audience of 80 Texas police chiefs, I asked, "Which one of you is the stupidest one in the room?" To my surprise, about 30 hands immediately shot up. Some of the Chiefs would see the others with their hand in the air and start arguing for the privilege of being the stupidest one in the room, "No way Bobby, you are just a half-wit; I am a complete and total idiot!" Well, those hands in the air blew the point I was trying to make: No one wants to look stupid.

Since that time, I have learned on those rare occasions when someone is willing to raise their hand and admit they are probably the stupidest person in the room, I have just identified the most pleasant and popular person in the room.

But most times, the question goes unanswered by my audiences. I was in Austin, Texas teaching full-day seminars with two Police Academy Recruit School classes, one on Monday and the next on Tuesday. As expected, no recruit raised his or her hand in either class. The third day, I presented an in-service seminar for the Police Department, and the entire department was represented: command staff, dispatchers, patrol, detectives, civilians, and supervisors.

I asked that audience, "Which one of you is the stupidest one in the room?" One hand shot up. I asked the gentleman, "What is your job title with the Department?"

He responded, "I am an Assistant Chief of Police!"

In that instant, I recognized my theory was confirmed: The willingness to be the stupidest person in the room is the key to getting promoted in a Police Department!

****

There is a bit of logic to my observation. Imagine you are part of a group of people in charge of hiring a new Police Chief. One candidate comes in and says, "I have got all the answers. My performance and record are flawless. I am the perfect man for the job, and you would be stupid not to hire someone as smart as me to be your new Chief!" The next candidate on the short list comes in and says, "Look, if you want to hire a perfect person, hire someone else. I am not perfect. I occasionally have said and done some stupid things. If you hire me, I am going to surround myself with lots of real smart people, and I am going to do my best not to make a mistake. But sometimes, I may appear to be the stupidest person in the room."

Now then, which candidate would you want to hire? Who would you rather work for? I think it is pretty clear. Some of the smartest people in the world are the ones who can admit they do not have all the answers! They are also the same ones who get hired, get promoted, and never fail to remember that no one ever wants to look stupid.

A Benefit of Admitting Stupidity

One of the great benefits that accrue to those who admit to being stupid is a lowering of expectations from your audiences. When those people drop the ball and look or say something stupid, what is the typical reaction they get from others? Often the reaction is, "Oh, that's O.K.; bless his heart; he is just a stupid idiot." They seem to get cut more slack and are given much more patience and consideration than those of us who just have to be the smartest one in the room. Now I ask, "Just who is the idiot in the room?"

Topic Shift for a Moment

Several years ago, a study was published which listed the greatest fears of Americans. Thousands of people were asked, "What do you fear?" Lots of fears and phobias made the list, but sitting atop the list is the number one fear of Americans. The one thing most people fear above all else—the fear of speaking in public!

I can assure you the study is wrong. People are not afraid of standing before an audience and speaking in public. I am a public speaker. I have taught courses in public speaking since 1980, and I am certain public speaking is not the number one fear.

I am convinced that the number one fear of Americans is the fear of looking stupid. Not that many people can admit it, so it is not surprising it didn't even make the list of "Top Fears."

People are not afraid of public speaking. They are afraid of looking stupid. You see, it is one thing to look stupid in front of your daughter as you guess wrong watching *Jeopardy* on TV. But how many of us are eager to appear on the show?

The grip of the fear of looking stupid is one of the greatest impediments to our success. For the fear of a stupid choice often prevents us from making the right choice. If I could do you a great favor, it would be to loosen the grip of the fear of looking stupid from around your shoulders because it has held you back in ways that are often unnoticed.

Here is an example. Let's say you are invited to a social event. You step into the room and see dozens of people you recognize. Then you spy a familiar face on the other side of the room. Unfortunately, you cannot remember that person's name. So, what do most of us do for the rest of the event in relation to that person across the room? Most choose to AVOID that person at all costs. Why? Because we have this fear of looking stupid that prevents us from going over and admitting we forgot their name. If the fear of looking stupid prevents us from taking a confident step toward that person, imagine the other ways, in other rooms, the fear of looking stupid has prevented us from confidently stepping forward.

Imagine I could lift the fear of looking stupid from your shoulders, and you were enrolled in my public speaking class. On the day you have to rise from your chair and step to the podium to deliver your speech for a grade, as you step forward, what are you afraid of? Certainly not tripping and falling on your face, in fact, you are fearless because you have no fear of looking stupid!

Now, let us say your public speaking classmate has got to be the smartest person in the room, just perfect in every way. As he steps forward to present his speech, is he afraid? You better believe he is filled with the fear that his facade may come crashing down. He fears his audience may see someone who isn't perfect in every way, and he is very afraid he may look or say something stupid!

If you want to become fearless, drop the fear of looking stupid right here and now. And if you want to improve your words remember: *No one wants to look stupid!*

PRINCIPLE THREE:
EVERYONE WANTS TO BE APPRECIATED

This is the most important of this chapter's principles. This one summarizes the previous two principles. If you forget those two, just remember this one: Everyone wants to be appreciated. Because if your audiences are showing appreciation, obviously you are doing something important, and you are not doing something stupid because people are showing their appreciation and saying, "Thank you, I appreciate your efforts!"

When working with police and government agencies, I often hear of problems with workforce morale and attitudes toward work in these organizations. Department leaders relate they are without the resources to raise pay, give promotions, or improve working conditions. With these limitations, they ask, "What can we do to improve attitudes and morale?"

The short answer: give them what they want. A study published by *The Advanced Management Journal* found that the top motivator of employee performance is "recognition for a job well done."

It appears the one thing people want most is the one thing they cannot ask for—some recognition and appreciation! To those seeking answers on how to improve current levels of motivation and morale in the workplace, the answer is decidedly effective, costs nothing, and is available in an inexhaustible supply for your use. I have yet to meet any employees in any organization who complain about getting TOO MUCH praise or appreciation from their supervisor and their organization!

Money is important. Status and position are important. But in my audiences, I find people who once left a high paying job and accepted a lower paying job because their new job allowed them to make important differences. Their lousy paying new job also gave them the opportunity to do important and sometimes heroic things of incredible service and self-sacrifice.

So, I encourage organizations to create both formal and informal ceremonies of appreciation. I encourage supervisors and individuals to actively seek out opportunities to give their colleagues what they want most from their work—a word of appreciation and an indication from a respected authority that what the employee does is important and praiseworthy. I encourage you to do the same!

PRINCIPLE FOUR:
NEVER CRITICIZE, CONDEMN OR COMPLAIN

I sense that if some of my participants embraced this chapter's fourth principle, we would never hear another word from their mouths. In seminars with a specific organization, I ask my participants to take another quick look around the room, and I ask, "Which one of you is the biggest complaining malcontent in your organization...who is it that seems to constantly be criticizing, condemning, or complaining about something in his life?"

He never raises his hand. Everyone in the room knows exactly who it is, but they are hesitant to point him out.

THE BIGGEST MALCONTENT IN THE ROOM

Once, I was conducting a two-day Leadership seminar with the Texas Tech University Police Department. Just before the seminar was to begin, the Chief gave me a challenge. He asked if I could identify, at the end of the seminar, which one of the 22 participants was his department's biggest complaining malcontent. I said, "Chief, I don't need 16 hours to figure that out. Just give me 16 seconds." I quickly looked into the eyes of the participants and observed posture and expression. I turned to the Chief and said, "The back row, far right, in the green plaid shirt."

"That's him!" the chief exclaimed.

I was tempted to turn to the class and ask each participant to write down the name of the biggest complaining malcontent in the room. I would have directed them to, "Fold your paper and pass it up to me."

I was willing to bet that twenty-one of the people in that room would have agreed with the Chief, but I was also willing to bet one of them would have seen it differently.

****

Complainers never see themselves as such. They believe they are just pointing out obvious problems. If I could get the complaining malcontents of the world to hear my words and act on my advice, it would be, "STOP IT! You are not doing yourself or the rest of us any favors with your constant complaints and observations of inadequacies and injustices."

The advice, "Never criticize, condemn, or complain," is not my advice. I borrowed it from someone else who published the advice in 1935. This advice is found on page nine of Dale Carnegie's book, *How to Win Friends & Influence People,* and it is his first principle of human relations.

Dale Carnegie also borrowed the principle from someone considered by some to be the greatest American writer. Dale Carnegie and others believed the author of this advice to be "the most perfect ruler of men the world has ever known," and as I learned later...he was the model example for the book, *How to Win Friends & Influence People.*

Who was Dale Carnegie's personal hero? With little prodding and a few guesses, audiences inevitably identify Abraham Lincoln.

Remember the seminar with the Texas Tech Police? At lunch, one of the participants drove home and retrieved an original 1932 publication by Dale Carnegie for my review. The officer eagerly gave me the book to keep for as long as I needed, the book's title— *The Unknown Lincoln.*

After reading this ten-year study of Lincoln by Carnegie, it was abundantly clear this book was the apparent model for his later publication, *How to Win Friends & Influence People*. Carnegie tells a story about young Lincoln. I take literary license in my retelling.

YOUNG LINCOLN

Lincoln was working in Springfield, Illinois as a lawyer and about to enter his first political campaign. Lincoln's opponent was a local politician and a confrontational type of man. Young Lincoln recognized the focus of many political campaigns is to criticize, condemn, and complain about your opponent. The strategy is to win, not because you are the best choice but because your audience is convinced your opponent is an idiot!

If you want to talk about someone who knows about the power of words, go directly to Abraham Lincoln. His words managed to change our world. Words are what lifted Abraham Lincoln from the darkness of the Kentucky wilderness to become a beacon of freedom for mankind. So, when Young Lincoln took a pen in his hand to criticize, condemn, and complain about his first political opponent, the finished product was an impressive collection of insult and condemnation. Lincoln submitted his anonymous letter for publication to the local paper, and it was eagerly published.

When the target of the scathing condemnation read the paper, he knew immediately who the anonymous author of those well-crafted words had to be. The enraged politician stormed into Lincoln's law office and demanded, "Did you write these words?" Lincoln replied in his soft Kentucky drawl with a hint of pride in his voice, "Yes sir, I did."

Lincoln's opponent then challenged, "Well, sir, you have defamed me in a most public manner. You leave me no choice but to defend my honor and challenge you to a duel to the death. Choose your weapon, Mr. Lincoln!"

Young Lincoln is a man of words. He is untrained and inexperienced in the military arts of death and dueling. However, public image and identity are critical to a politician, and Lincoln cannot risk having his political opponent label him as a coward. Lincoln feels he has no choice other than to accept the challenge. Lincoln chooses swords as the dueling weapon. The duel is on.

The two meet at the appointed place, a small sandbar that had formed in a bend of the river outside of town on the very western edge of current Western Civilization. Lincoln is positioned on one end of the sandbar, his opponent on the other end. Swords are raised, and just before they clash, the local lawmen ride in on horseback and demand the men break it up, explaining, "We may very well be on the western edge of civilization, but we are going to act like civilized folks. Now you two drop your weapons and return to your offices. And you, good citizens, return to your homes. The duel is not going to happen today or any other day."

Lincoln eagerly drops his weapon, quickly wades off of that sandbar, and strides up the steep riverbank. Atop solid ground, he lets out a big sigh of relief and says to his neighbors, "Friends, never criticize, condemn, or complain…heck, it'll get ya killed."

****

LINCOLN NEVER DID AGAIN

The truly unique thing about one of this country's greatest leaders is from that day forward he never did again. Since his death, there have been over 25,000 books written about Abraham Lincoln. If you were to read just about any chapter in any of those books, you would find abundant evidence that Lincoln did all he could to avoid criticizing, condemning, or complaining about the most important people in his life—the people he lived and worked with.

After his death, letters of criticism and condemnation were found in his office written and addressed to political and professional colleagues and adversaries but never sent.

His wife, Mary Todd Lincoln, was a highly critical, sharp-tongued, angry, opinionated, and vindictive woman. Today, she would probably be diagnosed as manic-depressive. Wide mood swings, excessive financial expenditures, deep funks of depression, jealousy, and erratic behavior were common with Mrs. Lincoln. However, Lincoln always treated her with the utmost value, dignity, and respect. His pet name for her was "Mother."

Once, a political colleague of Lincoln's came to his office and demanded Lincoln insist that Mrs. Lincoln offer a sincere apology for her remarks directed to him. Lincoln instead asked, "Sir, how long were you in the room with my wife, Mary?"

He replied, "Mr. President, I spoke to her for no more than two minutes, and I have never been so insulted in my entire life. That is why I demand a formal apology."

Lincoln drew a long breath, looked over his glasses, and sighed, "Before I do, for just one moment, please consider that I will spend the rest of my life with that woman."

The man hesitated, considered the prospect, and made a hasty retreat out the door saying, "Never mind, sir!"

Other Lincoln colleagues were often dismayed at the lack of discipline Lincoln would administer to his young sons Tad, Willie, and Robert. Important people engaged in important military and political discussions were appalled to find their discussions at the White House interrupted by Lincoln's loud and unruly sons, sometimes escorted by pet goats and dogs. Cabinet members would look pleadingly into Lincoln's eyes silently imploring him to do something about his damn kids' interruptions. But Lincoln, as always, remained oblivious to the boys' faults. Lincoln decided to save the honor of criticism for the many others in his sons' future who would be eager for the opportunity.

Lincoln could fire a general without criticizing the officer's performance. General George McClellan's removal as General of the Union Army is just one example. Lincoln was long frustrated that his General would not take the fight to the South. Finally, his patience at an end, he summoned the General to the White House. Lincoln said, "General, I need your help. We have a big problem, and I believe you are the only person I can turn to for help. Here is the problem: We need a bigger army. It is going to take military leaders to lead the great army that is going to save the Union. General, no one in uniform is better at taking men and turning them into soldiers than you. No one is better at taking soldiers and turning them into leaders. General, may I ask that you immediately take over as Commandant of West Point and help create the leaders who are going to save the union? Would you do your country this great favor?"

Lincoln learned the lessons of saying the wrong thing to the wrong person early in his political career on a sandbar in a river. The next time you have a five-dollar bill in your hand, take a good hard look into the eyes of Abraham Lincoln, and remember to never criticize, condemn, or complain. It will probably be the best five-dollar advice you get that day or any other day in your efforts to say the right words at the right time.

My readers, I ask if you get nothing else out of this book, please remember these universal principles:

Everyone wants to be important.
No one wants to look stupid.
Everyone wants to be appreciated.
Never criticize, condemn or complain.

If you embrace just these four principles to guide your words, life may not get better for you, but I can guarantee life will get better for the most important people in your life!

Chapter Two Review:
Your Philosophy of Human Interaction

A philosophy is a set of guiding principles.

The Idiot's Philosophy of Human Interaction:
 I talk to people the way they talk to me!

Every religion suggests a version of The Golden Rule:
 Do unto others as you would have others do unto you.

Using your expectations to guide your interactions will
 cause problems for you.

The Platinum Rule:
 Treat people better than they expect,
 and you can expect to be treated better!

Four Universal Principles of Human Interaction:
 ❑ *Everyone Wants to Be Important.*
 ❑ *No One Wants to Look Stupid.*
 ❑ *Everyone Wants to Be Appreciated.*
 ❑ *Never Criticize, Condemn, or Complain.*

The number one fear of Americans: *The Fear of Looking
 Stupid.*

The willingness to admit to your stupidity can enhance your
 popularity, lower expectations, and get you promoted.

The top motivator of employee performance is
 recognition for a job well done.

No one complains about receiving too much appreciation.

THREE
Your Most Important Verbal Skill

With a five-dollar bill in my hand, I offer a challenge to my seminar participants, "I will give this five-dollar bill to the first one of you to identify what I believe is Your Most Important Verbal Skill."

You may be like of lot of my participants, certain you know the answer that wins the five-dollar bill. I often see several eager hands in the air, but no matter which person I choose to answer, I almost always get the same guess—listening.

I applaud that answer, congratulate them for their answer's emphasis on a receiving skill as being most important, and then give the participant a "high five" but not my five-dollar bill. I am sorry to report to my now disappointed participant that I do not believe listening to be your most important of the important verbal skills we endeavor to develop.

I ask for another guess. The most common second guess is eye contact. Nice guess. But again, unfortunately, no! It is not facial expression, vocal tone, gesture, kinesics, chronemics, or any other of the host of nonverbal skills. Your most important verbal skill cannot be one of the nonverbal skills. Nonverbal means not of words and verbal skills must involve words.

Symbolic Verbal Interaction

Let me define what I teach. I define communication as symbolic interaction. We interact with symbols when we read, listen, write, and speak words. A large part of our early education is dedicated to becoming skilled at using words. The four verbal skills include two sending (speak and write) sets of skills and two receiving (read and listen) sets of skills. My professional emphasis has always been in symbolic interaction using the spoken word.

Do you want to try another guess? If not, let me give you two specific examples of the type of verbal skills I am hoping you would guess as your most important.

THE WORLD'S GREATEST

I am a former university professor. It was a nice job, and I worked with some terrific colleagues and students.

The best part and the worst part of any job are the people you work with. There is one colleague I miss more than almost anything else about my old job. This particular 80 year-old gentleman I met only a few months prior to my leaving the University. His name is Ralph Eubanks, Ph.D.

I met Ralph after he approached my boss, the Chair of the Department of Speech Communication, at the university where I was teaching. He introduced himself as a retired professor emeritus from a Florida university who had recently settled in Arkansas to be closer to his son and family. He asked if he could serve as a volunteer professor to our department, faculty, and students. Ralph was welcomed to the faculty.

In the shortest time possible, Ralph became the most popular person in our department. Everyone, from 18 year-old college students to 50 year-old professors, just loved talking to Ralph. I couldn't wait to introduce my family to this new colleague who everyone loved to talk to.

Then the social scientist in me began wondering—what exactly is Ralph doing? He certainly is getting a different reaction from his audiences. He must be doing something different with his words.

To discover his secret, I started to observe his daily interactions with a wide variety of audiences. I quickly came to an obvious conclusion: Ralph is the "World's Greatest" at the Art of Giving a Compliment. After every conversation I observed, I would see his audiences walk away feeling better about themselves and circumstances—every time!

One day, soon after coming to this epiphany, I saw Ralph walk by my office door, and I invited him to step into my office for a visit. I explained to Ralph that I had been observing his interactions with others on campus. I told him I had discovered that he does something with his words better than anyone else I had ever observed. "In fact," I said, "you, sir, are a model of communication excellence for our students and a mentor to this humble communication professor. Ralph, do you know what you are the absolute best at doing with your words?"

Ralph shook his head, no. I instantly realized that he is what we in academia call "unconsciously competent." He does it skillfully but is unaware he is doing it! I have since forced myself to become more consciously competent in this area of verbal fluency that comes naturally to Ralph. Some of us are unconsciously competent and still others are consciously incompetent in offering words of encouragement, recognition, and appreciation.

"Ralph, you are the World's Greatest at Giving Compliments," I said. "Everyone you talk to walks away feeling better about themselves."

Now, just watch how good Ralph truly is. His 80 year-old eyes dropped to the floor and slowly rose again until they locked onto my brown eyes. Ralph said, "Brian, what you just said to me, why I believe that was the nicest thing anyone has ever said to me in my entire life!"

You see just how good Ralph is. I give him a compliment, and he immediately tops my compliment with an even bigger one. But I have learned at the foot of the Master. I then proclaimed, "Ralph, that was just about the nicest thing anyone has ever said to me!"

Ralph said, "Brian, you are a wonderful man."

I said, "Ralph, you are a warm, terrific human being."

He added, "Brian, in your work with law enforcement, I just know you are making important differences in important people's lives."

I said, "Me? Ralph, I bet the planet Earth is a completely different place having you on it for the past eighty years!"

****

Another Verbal Skill

Earlier, I told you I would give you two examples of specific types of verbal skills. Let's look at another verbal skill, the complete opposite of a compliment. You may know people in your own life, people like Ralph who are practiced, skilled, and willing to use their words to create a specific reaction from their audiences, but they seek the complete opposite reaction. They are "consciously competent" at using their words to make people feel unimportant, stupid, or unappreciated, not to encourage the human spirit but to condemn and destroy it. There are some in my audiences who take a great deal of pride in their ability to insult. They proudly and skillfully demean those unfortunate souls who are targets of their criticism, condemnation, and complaints as if that ability was something to be proud of.

I do not believe insulting or complimenting people is your most important communication skill. Neither is listening or any of the nonverbal skills. The territory is getting smaller. Would you like to try another guess?

A common guess at this point is persuasion: the ability to use words to change thinking and attitudes. I applaud that guess. Our success is largely dependent on getting people to see things as we do, to change thinking and attitudes. However, there is one skill that is more sophisticated and critical than your ability to successfully persuade audiences to accept your propositions.

Quick example. Here is a persuasive proposition: *Everyone should exercise for thirty minutes each day.*

I ask my audiences, "How many of you think I could successfully persuade everyone in this audience to accept that proposition?" Some participants frown and shake their heads as if to say, "No way." Others read the proposition as stated—everyone SHOULD exercise thirty minutes each day. Most will agree with that and say, "Well, sure! You can do that, convince them they *should*." Their emphasis indicates they recognize there is a much more difficult task yet to accomplish: getting people to do what you want them to do, to change behavior.

Some participants now confidently say, "Motivating Action must be what you believe to be your most important verbal skill!" Once again, I disappoint and indicate no. There is still yet another verbal skill I believe to be your most important.

The Four Best Hints

Here are the four best hints I offer as clues to what I believe is your most important verbal skill:
1. It is the central competency. If you endeavor to become a better listener, persuader, or motivator, you had better be skilled at this specific verbal skill.
2. It is what I have been doing during the past several pages.
3. The less mature you are, the more likely it is you will use this specific verbal skill.
4. It is the universal characteristic of successful people.

Now, with those four hints, the answer should be obvious, or perhaps not. I offer a five-dollar prize for guessing what I think is your most important verbal skill at every seminar I facilitate, and I very rarely lose my picture of Abraham Lincoln.

What do I believe is your most important verbal skill? The answer is the question! Asking Questions—the Skill of Inquiry—I argue is Your Most Important Verbal Skill.

Remember the first of the four hints? Asking questions is the central competency. If you endeavor to become a better listener, persuader, or motivator, you had better be skilled at asking questions. You know someone is listening if they ask questions of clarification or elaboration. And if you endeavor to persuade or motivate, an important first step is to start asking some important questions about why your audience sees things a bit differently than you.

The second hint indicated that I had been specifically using the skill during the previous few pages. The skill I had been using was Asking Questions. The question I asked was, "What do you think is your most important verbal skill?" Asking a question is a great way to get audience participation and unique insights into their opinions, their views, their values, and their priorities. With those answers, I am in a much better position to get them marching out that door in the direction I suggest!

The third hint was, "The less mature you are, the more likely you are to use this specific verbal skill." Have you ever spent any time with a three year-old child? Pretty obvious, isn't it? Asking questions certainly is important to a three year-old! It is as if they are on the game show *Jeopardy!* Everything out of a contestant's mouth must be in the form of a question. Everyone also recognizes a three year-old wants to know the answer to one specific question above all others. You know the question, the three-letter word repeated endlessly from the lips of every three year-old: WHY?

Soon after I discovered the absolute central position of asking questions in competent interaction, supporting evidence began to appear everywhere, including my breakfast table.

THAT IS A GOOD QUESTION

Early one morning, after retrieving my newspaper, I slipped into my seat at the breakfast table to begin my day. Through blurry eyes, I was greeted by the sight of my then three year-old daughter, Kendall, staring at me from across the table. She sat across the table staring at me with one tiny hand covering one of her beautiful brown eyes.

Some people describe me as something of a grump in the morning. This morning I did what I would do most any morning with anyone staring at me at 6:20 a.m., I ignored her. I focused my eyes on my cereal bowl and the sports page. As I worked my way through my bowl of Froot Loops and the newspaper, I could see Kendall out of the corner of my eye. She continued to concentrate on my face as she covered both eyes and then uncovered one eye. She continued to stare and cover one eye and then the other until I finally barked my first words of the day, "What is it? What is with the eye covering/uncovering thing you are doing there? Huh?"

She said, "Dad, I am looking at you with just this one eye…O.K.?" I nodded in impatient agreement as she covered her other eye. She then covered both eyes. Then, as she uncovered her other eye, she said, "Now Dad, I am looking at you with this one eye, and I still see just one of you. My question is, Why—as she uncovered both eyes—why don't I see two of you now that I am looking with two eyes…Dad?"

****

Now, that is the kind of question that can only come from a three year-old. Kendall is now 16 years old. Have you ever been around a 16 year-old? Something changes in the way they choose to interact with the world. Why don't you ever hear a 16 year-old ask a question? My audiences say it is because they think they know it all!

You bet. When you know it all, you know you can't ask anyone a question. Because if you did ask a question, you would demonstrate that you do not have all the answers! With one question, you prove your ignorance, often to the very audiences you worked so hard to convince that you know all the answers. Being the smartest person in the room, the one with all the answers, must be a tough spot. You can't use your most important verbal skill.

We have an advantage at age three which we lose by age sixteen. The advantage you have at three years old is that you know you are not the smartest in the room. You feel free to demand logical explanations for why things are the way they are from anyone else in the room! I think part of the charm of young children is they make us feel real smart when we are with them.

The final hint I offered was, "Your most important skill is the universal characteristic of successful people." Successful people ask for success. They ask, and they ask, and they ask until one day...they get what they want!

The Tools of Inquiry

This chapter used to be the first lecture of my freshman level communication course at the University. At the end of the first day, I would introduce my students to the six journalistic tools of reporting:

WHO   WHAT   WHEN   WHERE   WHY   HOW

I told my university students, "As you march through life, keep these six questions handy. In almost any social situation, asking questions is likely to be your most appropriate response to life's most difficult situations." As they search for the right words, I suggested those words are usually in the form of the right question.

If you find yourself in a difficult social situation and don't know exactly what to say, pull out your most important communication skill and start asking questions!

I also assured my college freshmen that they are going to quickly forget the answers to the questions on the hundreds of exams they will take over the coming years, but that is O.K. Years from now, they will emerge with a degree in hand, but it will not be stuffed with ready answers. That is O.K. too. We professors are here to help make you better critical thinkers, better problem solvers, and better prepared to successfully function in a complex world. The goal isn't to fill your head up with answers but rather to help you to ask the right questions!

You Can Only Ask One Question

At the conclusion of my first day lecture, I would give my students their first class assignment—ask questions! The assignment has the restriction that for the next two days, all they can do is ask questions; they cannot tell anybody anything. Everything coming out of their mouth has to be in the form of a question. But before they stand and march, there is one further restriction. My students are required to use only one of the six tools of inquiry, and only one. Choose the one and march:

WHO   WHAT   WHEN   WHERE   WHY   HOW

There are six choices. Interestingly, the vast majority of my university students all chose the same question to ask.

If you are like the vast majority of people, you would select the same question, the question WHY.

I applaud that choice. The question WHY is the impetus for every theory and hypothesis ever postulated! The connection between the theoretic world and the real world is the question WHY. We march through life constantly creating personal theories of why things are the way they are.

You may ask why some people are the most successful in your profession. You posit a theory, and that explanation guides you through your professional life, hopefully successfully. Let us hope you have a good, valid, reliable, and practical theory of professional success, marital success, parental success, and financial success.

There is a Problem with the Question Why

Theories are important, and everyone just naturally wants to know the answer to questions of WHY. But there is a bit of a problem with the question WHY. If you are a supervisor or a parent, then you have often faced the problems associated with posing the question WHY. Those of you in a position of authority have some expectations about the performance of those you supervise. Given that you are evaluated on the performance of your subordinates, it is natural for you to have a number of expectations about their performance. Sometimes they meet your expectations, and sometimes they do not. Supervisors also learn the higher your expectations, the easier it is for others to fail to meet your expectations.

When those cases of failed expectations arise, we often invite our subordinates into our office to explain, "WHY? Why can't you meet my performance expectations?" When supervisors ask that question, in those circumstances, do they receive an explanation? Rarely. The most likely response is one of feigned ignorance or possibly a litany of excuses, rationalizations, and justifications involving events completely out of their control. You asked, "Why?" in the hopes of a logical explanation, and often you receive anything but an answer to your question.

The Burden of Expectations

My young daughter, Kendall, has been forced to march through her entire life with one particularly heavy burden. Her particular burden is this one: Her parents think her big sister, Lauren, is just about perfect in every way! Kendall shoulders a burden of high expectations set by a predecessor. You may be familiar with the burden in your professional lives. Maybe it has happened in your household like it happened in ours. When Lauren was born, we were young parents, and I had never held an infant in my hands until they handed her to me, moments after her birth, to present to her mother! I had zero expectations. Every little thing was new and everything seemed perfect about this baby. And, as the years went by, everything rolled along perfectly. We decided to add to our perfect little family. Expectations awaited the arrival of our second child, expectations that didn't burden our first-born.

My daughters are very different in a number of ways. The fact that Lauren is cooperative and Kendall is competitive is just one of a number of differences. I started noticing differences in Melissa's pregnancy even before Kendall was born, and my expectations have been jolted almost every day since. However, I was always delighted to hear Kendall's teachers all describe her in the same way they had once described her sister: bright student at the top of the class, helpful, cooperative, and gets along wonderfully with all the other students in the classroom!

Apparently, my young daughter's competitiveness on the athletic fields was being successfully applied in her classrooms. Things flowed along perfectly for years. I learned, time and again, that two daughters can be as different as they can be and still perfect in every way.

LET ME ASK YOU JUST ONE QUESTION

Then one day, I held Kendall's interim report card in my hand, and I saw something on it I had never seen in all my years as supervisor of academics in my household. I saw a poor grade in one of my daughter's 5th grade studies! By now, her older sister was in the 9th grade, and I had never seen anything other than A's and an occasional B. I had never seen a lousy grade on either of my daughter's report cards. But there it was. I rubbed my incredulous eyes, and it was still there, Mathematics: D+.

There I sat in my small home office. Across the hall, my daughter was in her bedroom studying. I hollered out, "Kendall, get in here right now!" She appeared, and I said, "I am looking at your interim report card, and I see a lousy grade reported in your Math class. Let me ask you one simple little question!"

Which question naturally rises to my lips? Of course, the one question everyone always wants answered: WHY? I could have asked, "Why, young lady, am I looking at a lousy grade on this report card, why are you failing, why can't you be more like…?"

You haven't met my young daughter, and you do not know what she looks like. But you know the look on her face if she was faced with a demand for an explanation. You also know the feeling in the pit of her stomach if her Ph.D. father towered above her demanding to know, "Why have you violated my expectations in your performance!"

Now, imagine how different that interaction would be if after I said, "Let me ask you one question," I asked not WHY but instead asked,

"HOW can I help you…

HOW can we work together…

HOW can we ensure your success together?"

✳✳

I imagine any little girl would prefer a HOW question to a WHY question in that situation. I imagine the look on her face and the feeling in her stomach would improve with an offer of assistance as opposed to a demand for an explanation.

One of the problems with questions of WHY is they are sometimes accusatory and often create defensiveness in audiences. The defensiveness produced by demands to know, "Why have my expectations been violated?" result in answers of ignorance, rationalization, and justification.

The Role of Discovery and Leadership

I remind supervisors and parents that their roles are not ones of explanation—to learn WHY things are. Their roles are ones of discovery and leadership—to show HOW things can be! Parents, supervisors, coaches and teachers are a source of answers to the important questions of HOW. Leaders, with their wisdom and experience, can lead others down the path to success by demonstrating HOW!

The questions of WHY also have the inherent problem of being speculative and often impossible to answer. We search for answers to WHY things are the way they are: Why are things so screwed up? Why me? Why now? Why this? We lay awake at night, staring at the ceiling, repeatedly asking ourselves unanswerable questions of WHY.

Instead, we should be focused on the question that can be answered. HOW am I going to respond? HOW am I going to be successful tomorrow? HOW can I make important differences in the lives of others? HOW can I enhance my image, my relationships, and my success in this world?

WHY questions are focused on the past and speculative. HOW questions are pragmatic questions focused on the future.

Four Questions Every Audience Wants Answered

Dale Carnegie and I have something in common. We both started out as public speaking instructors. We both hoped, as young men, to someday help others present their messages in public settings to large audiences.

We both learned that our students rarely, if ever, actually had opportunities to apply their lessons in public speaking. Just about everyone appears before the public and speaks. However, the audience is often only one person. Over the years, I have discovered that many of the principles that apply to educating, persuading and motivating large audiences also apply when you have an audience of only one.

One thing I have learned about audiences of 1001 and audiences of only one person is they both want answers to questions. I have also learned that every audience is looking to the speaker to reduce their uncertainty about four specific questions.

I used to evaluate my public speaking students on how well their introduction answered the four questions every audience wants answered.

Who Are You?

The first of the four questions is, "Who are you?" And I do not mean your audience wants your name, rank, and serial number. Audiences want to know who are you to them. Are you here to serve and protect me, or are you here to threaten and bully me? Are you on my side or against me? Are you here to insult me and make me feel stupid, or are you here to encourage me and make me feel important? Are you here to remind me of my incompetence, or are you going to help me be successful? Just exactly who are you to me?

Public speakers are encouraged to share information but to also share of themselves. Aristotle spoke of audience identification. Successful orators manage to get their audiences to identify with the speaker. Ethos, trust, and credibility are all related to the idea of being seen as one who the audience can relate to and identify with.

In my seminars, I almost always include the same two things in my introductory remarks. First, I include some discussion of my daughters being so surprisingly different from one another. Second, I admit I sometimes say and do some stupid things. While many of my participants can relate to the first, everyone can identify with the second.

WHY IS THIS HAPPENING?

Everyone, starting before the age of three, demands to know the answer to this question immediately! Every audience wants to know, "Why am I listening to your words?"

You will recall, I had the privilege of sharing my message with 1500 Texas Police Chiefs over a period of two years. At a break, I asked them to answer this question on a brief survey:

What is the single most frustrating and irritating thing a citizen can say to a police officer during a traffic stop?

Predictably, the number one response was this:

"Why aren't you out there catching real criminals instead of hassling minor traffic violators?"

As I collected hundreds of responses, I was at first a bit surprised and then mildly disappointed when some suggested this was the most irritating thing officers hear:

"Why did you pull me over?"

I was surprised because that is the single most predictable question on the lips of any participant in a public presentation. Public speakers are encouraged to relate early why this occasion was selected to share these words, why this topic, and why this audience should pay attention to their words. Every three year-old wants the answer to the question WHY. Students and seminar participants all agree if they could ask just one question, it would be the question WHY. So, why any professional law enforcement officer is irritated when his audience demands to know, "WHY ME?" surprises me.

I am a bit disappointed because my research tells me that the recommended Seven Steps of Violator Contact (taught in police academies in the state of Texas) includes, in Step Two, a simple rhetorical strategy that absolutely prevents an audience from asking that question. The rhetorical strategy is to tell them WHY up front so that your audience does not feel compelled to ask! So, if any officer is irritated by the question, I can assume they are irritating their supervisors by failing to follow policy and failing to tell the violator WHY this is happening.

Some officers feel compelled to ask the violator, "Do you know why I pulled you over?" I can only surmise a confession or correct guess would factor into the officer's final decision of whether to ticket or not. But I know me, and I know what I know. And I know if an officer asked me, "Do you know why I pulled you over, sir?" I would be compelled to ask, "Officer, if you do not know why you pulled me over, how can you expect me to know? It is your traffic stop. You tell me WHY!"

Well, I'm probably going to get a ticket, but you get my point.

WHAT IS IN IT FOR ME?

The third question every audience wants answered is the one above. If you are in the persuasion business, then you are in the business of answering this question, "What's in it for me?" above all others. People are selfish, egocentric beings whose survival needs are of primary interest, and every situation is assessed on whether cooperation is in their personal best interest.

Confessions to capital murder, on the surface, would never appear to be in anyone's best interest, particularly those related to personal survival. However, a skilled interrogator can often persuade his audience that confession is, in this circumstance, in that suspect's best interest. People are selfish and will do what they believe is best for them.

If you can persuade your audience their cooperation will make them an important person, make them look smart, make them feel appreciated, and serve their best interest, you may be surprised how cooperative difficult people can become.

What is Going to Happen?

In public speaking, this is called a preview. For example, "We will be covering four important questions in today's discussion."

The preview is the process of setting expectations for audiences about WHAT will happen during the presentation. Public speakers seek to establish expectations about their message, their audience, and the benefits of their audience's cooperation.

Here are four questions every audience wants answered:

Who are you?
Why is this happening?
What is in it for me?
What is going to happen?

One More for the Thumb

When I critiqued student speeches, the evaluation of their introduction was mostly a consideration of how well the speaker answered the four questions above. A good introduction will answer all four questions every audience wants answered.

There is one more question the most important people in your life want you to answer—the one question that everyone wants answered every day of his or her life. If you are an important person, then you have people looking to you to answer this one question for them. And even if you answered the question 12 times yesterday, they will want you to answer the question 13 times today. What is the one question the important people in your life want answered every day?

Am I O.K.?

Everyone wants to be important. No one wants to look stupid. Everyone wants to be appreciated, and everyone wants to be told they are O.K. No wonder everyone wants to talk to my friend,

Ralph. He gives the answer everyone wants to the one question everyone wants answered!

No wonder I try and convince both my daughters I think they are not only O.K. but perfect in every way. I know if they are not convinced the most important man in their young lives thinks they are O.K., young women will seek someone else who will give them the answer they want.

The Five Word Question That Answers All Five Questions

In my seminars, it takes me several minutes to answer all five of the questions I know my audience wants answered. I also know a way I can answer all of my audience's important questions by asking one five-word question.

If you can guess the answer to the riddle, you deserve a spot at the top of my class and recognition as My Favorite Student. What is the magic five-word question that answers all five of the questions below?

Who are you?
Why is this happening?
What is in it for me?
What is going to happen?
And even: Am I O.K.?

How can I help you find the answer to the riddle? Simply re-read the first five words of the previous sentence to find the answer!

How can I help you? That five-word question answers the questions of who I am, why is this happening, what's in it for you, and what is going to happen! No wonder I love working with police officers in my seminars. I am working with professionals who not only ASK this most important of important questions but are often placed in the unique position to ANSWER this question. They answer: Here is how I am going to help you! What follows is occasionally something remarkably heroic. The unasked question, "Am I O.K.?" is answered with, "Of course. I am here to help you!"

THE MOST IMPORTANT PERSON YOU TALK TO

After keeping my five dollar bill earlier in my seminars, I now reach deep into my pocket and offer my participants TWO pictures of Abraham Lincoln if one of them can raise their hand and answer this question: Who is the most important person you talk to?

Often, a guess I hear is, "The person you are talking to!" While the guess is technically correct, it's not the one I am looking for. I understand the answer above was one of Mary Kay's, of cosmetic fame, favorite principles. I wish I could offer a pink Cadillac for that answer, but I cannot.

But I can offer two pictures of Lincoln for the answer— yourself! And to the first participant to say, "You (yourself) are the most important person you talk to," I reach deep into my wallet and produce two shiny pennies with a picture of Lincoln on each. I remind the winner not to feel short-changed because there are actually FOUR pictures of Lincoln on two pennies (on the back of each penny is a teenie weenie Abe sitting inside the Memorial).

THE TWO-CENT ANSWER

You are the most important person you talk to! You argue with yourself, debate, encourage, persuade, insult, compliment, and motivate yourself. The most important conversations you have are the ones you have with yourself, and successful people manage that one conversation better than any other. They focus not on handy justification for their failures, instead they spend their time figuring out HOW to be successful. They are "self-motivated," meaning they do a great job of talking themselves into doing the things that lead to success.

Thomas Edison, on the failure of his 200th attempt to invent a functioning light bulb, told himself, "Brilliant! I have successfully discovered the 200th way NOT to invent the light bulb!"

You probably already know you should exercise for thirty minutes every day, right? You know you should be eating healthy, right? But how many of us can successfully persuade and motivate the one audience we are with 24 hours, each and every day, to do the right thing? And if we cannot successfully motivate that audience to do what is in our own selfish best interest, how can we hope to motivate the other important audiences in our lives to do the right thing?

Given that YOU are the most important person you talk to, and asking questions is your most important verbal skill, it would behoove each of you to ask yourself some questions.

Ask Yourself Some Questions

Below are a number of questions competent communicators constantly ask themselves about their interactions with others. Academics describe these people as "high self-monitors."

Twenty Questions to Ask Yourself:
1. Do I talk too much?
2. Do I complain too much?
3. Am I often sarcastic?
4. Is my language occasionally offensive?
5. Do I often encourage others?
6. Do I express appreciation often?
7. Do I gladly point out the flaws in others?
8. Do I talk too much about myself, my partner,
     my health, my problems, my needs,
     my achievements, my religion, my job, my kids,
     my boss, my dog, my friends, my hobbies,
     my politics, etc.?

9. Do I compliment others often?
10. Do I talk poorly about other people?
11. Do I regret what I have said?
12. Can I give constructive criticism?
13. Do I take criticism constructively?
14. Do I call people names?
15. Do I argue needlessly with important people?
16. Do I interrupt others when they are speaking?
17. Do I lie about myself when I could tell the truth?
18. Am I occasionally cruelly honest to others?
19. Can I give an appropriate apology?
20. Do I take absolute responsibility for my words?

In my seminars, I ask my participants to quickly try and answer just three questions about what they can do to communicate more effectively:

1. What can you QUIT DOING with your words?
2. What can you START DOING with your words?
3. What should you REMEMBER about your words?

The answers to the previous 20 questions and the answers to these three questions should be different for each participant. However, I have some suggestions for all participants.

QUIT DOING THAT

Some folks don't need to start anything new at all. For some, if they would immediately just STOP doing some of the things they do with their words, they would become more competent with their words. Review the 20 questions above to decide what you may need to quit doing in your interactions with others.

Start Doing This

Actively seek out opportunities to offer a kind word of encouragement and recognition to those who undeniably deserve it. Feed words of support to audiences possibly starving for an occasional word of appreciation. Give your audiences the one thing they want to hear more than anything else: You are O.K.!

Remember This

Asking questions is your most important verbal skill. Your effort to say just the right words is usually an effort to find just the right question. And that question is often just these five words: How can I help you?

CHAPTER THREE REVIEW:
YOUR MOST IMPORTANT VERBAL SKILL

Asking questions is Your Most Important Verbal Skill.

Good listeners, persuaders, motivators, and creative thinkers ask good questions.

Questions can get your audience involved and participating.

We lose our child-like willingness to ask questions.

The Fear of Looking Stupid prevents us from asking important questions.

Believing you have all the answers prevents you from asking important questions.

The Tools of Inquiry:
Who, What, When, Where, Why, and How

Questions demanding explanation create defensiveness.

The roles of leaders and parents are to demonstrate HOW, not to ask, "WHY?"

Five Questions Everyone Wants Answered:
- ❑ *Who are you?*
- ❑ *Why is this happening?*
- ❑ *What is in it for me?*
- ❑ *What is going to happen?*
- ❑ *Am I O.K.?*

The Five-Word Question That Answers All Five Questions:
How can I help you?

You are the most important person you talk to.

The right words are often found in the form of a question.

FOUR
The Art of Conversation

My second lecture to freshman university students was always on the Art of Conversation. Most professional audiences I speak to are well versed in the art of social interaction, and I include this lecture in only some of my seminars.

At the University, my students were often 18 year-old college freshmen away from family and friends for the first time. I was eager to share these lessons on mastering the art of conversation.

Most of my students did not have much difficulty talking to people just like them. They were completely at ease with familiar faces and faces similar to their own. Universities are teeming with unfamiliar faces, many from other communities, some from the other side of their towns, some from the other side of the world, and some who look as if they came from another planet.

For a number of college freshman, their social posture is to keep their head down, eyes diverted, mouth shut, and feet moving. That social posture is a problem for young freshmen embarking on a journey through the halls of higher education.

I warned my students, "If you leave this campus and still have difficulty talking with people who are different than you, the world of academia has a label for you."

A Social Retard

If you are unable to talk to people who are different than you,
    People who look different than you,
    People who talk different than you,
    People who dress different than you,
    People who think different than you,
    People who are different than you,
    Then you are going be retarded socially.

This is a Test

Before we examine the traits of Master Conversationalists, let's take a test to measure your likely aptitude for Master's status in social conversation:
    1. Do you like people?
    2. Do you generally find people to be entertaining, helpful, likeable, and enlightening?
    3. Do you find people to be encouraging and inspiring?
    4. Do you consider yourself to be somewhat shy?

If you answer YES to all four questions…congratulations, you are already well on your way to mastering social conversation, especially if you said YES to the fourth question. Those who say NO to question number four are often the same ones who say, "Heck no, I do not have a shy bone in my body. I can talk all day long. I can talk your ear off! I can tell you everything you need to know about anything."

Great Conversationalists Give
Their Audiences What They Want

Some of those who say NO to question four certainly can talk, but they find it impossible to converse. Eighty percent of us say we are at least somewhat shy. Great Conversationalists make the conversation about their audience. They put the spotlight on others, and they get others to talk about themselves. Those of us who consider ourselves somewhat shy are delighted to give our audiences what they want—a voice in the conversation!

YOUR HOMEWORK ASSIGNMENT

An assignment I often gave my college freshmen was: "Go out and initiate as many social conversations as possible over the next two days with people different than you. Write up a brief summary of your three most interesting conversations, and turn that in for credit next class period. Stand and March!"

Some of my students were delighted to receive such an easy assignment. Others received the assignment with a look of terror on their faces. And what were they were afraid of? I suspect it was the fear of looking stupid.

Before I dismissed them, I'd share a few characteristics and principles that guide master conversationalists in their social interactions.

TIPS FROM MASTER CONVERSATIONALISTS

ALWAYS MAKE THE OTHER PERSON FEEL IMPORTANT

Although there are many ways we can make others feel important, I ask my participants, "What is the quickest, simplest, and easiest way to make someone feel important?"

This is one of the most difficult questions for my audiences to guess the answer. Eventually, someone recognizes the quickest way to make someone feel important is to ASK for some help!

Everyone wants to be important, and helping others is a quick and easy way to feel important. Those who can never ask for any help are missing opportunities to make people feel important. A number of students reported fascinating conversations that began with the student simply asking for campus directions.

I reminded my young college students that many of them were going to be around this campus for six, seven, maybe more years completing their undergraduate degree. Maybe, there were people on this very campus eager to give students direction to things other than the student union. Maybe, I advised, if you asked for some help, you just might get it!

Lauren, my college bound daughter who I had no advice for, gets it. She makes it a point, early in the semester, to introduce herself to her professors in their office. She returns and asks for help with her studies whenever she needs it. Is that in her best interest? As a former professor, I know that it is because I know professors like to look smart, feel important, and help students. And, as her father, I am delighted to learn she is on schedule to complete her pre-med degree in less than the four years it took her father to complete his speech degree.

REPEAT NAMES OFTEN

I ask my audiences, "How many of you have ever said to yourself: I am great at remembering faces, but I cannot remember people's names?" Typically, everyone in the room raises their hand or nods in agreement.

I feign surprise and exclaim, "None of you are better at remembering names then faces?" Have you ever had someone say to you, "I don't recognize your face, but I know your name"? Of course not! All of us are better at remembering faces than names. Faces are visible and they are all so very different. But names are only auditory, verbal, transparent, and gone in a moment. No wonder it is so much easier to remember faces, and no wonder nametags are so popular!

As soon as we tell ourselves we can't do something, guess what? We can't. We don't remember names because we aren't trying. And we don't try because it is hard.

Great Conversationalists know this about remembering names. As soon as they get the opportunity, they start repeating the new name until it isn't new anymore.

INTERESTING PEOPLE ARE INTERESTED PEOPLE

Have you ever received a phone call and asked the caller, "How was your day?" and then wished you hadn't asked? You just know for the next 20 minutes you are going to have to listen to that person prattle on endlessly about the neurotic nuances of every aspect of their pitiful life and forced to listen as they go on and on criticizing, condemning, and complaining about any and everything.

Most of us have been stuck in that situation, stuck with a phone to our ear with nothing to say other than, "Uh huh." Some will admit to gently setting the phone down and walking away for a few minutes. Later, they re-join the "conversation" with, "Uh Huh."

Obviously, this isn't a very interesting conversation. The other person isn't asking any questions or showing any interest in others, so we are free to walk away. If you want to become a more interesting conversationalist, become more interested.

EASILY COMPLIMENT OTHERS

I learned this tip from observing my former colleague, Ralph. I tell my students if the assignment of conversations intimidates you, use this tip exclusively. Find people who deserve a sincere compliment and build your conversation from there.

Imagine this scene—a young college student knocks on the door of an older couple up the block from where the student lives with his or her roommates. Although they live near one another, neither neighbor has been introduced. Motivated by the assignment, the student speaks to the woman who opens the door. "Good afternoon, I am your neighbor from down the street. I am so impressed by the effort you put into your yard. Every day, I tell myself it is the prettiest yard in the neighborhood. Today, I thought I would stop to tell you that and introduce myself. It is a pleasure to finally meet you; I am…"

Now, what are the odds that woman will slam the door in the student's face? Some young students and others have that fear.

After the students complete the assignment and return to class, I ask them to write down the biggest lesson learned from completing this assignment. Over the years, I consistently saw the same lessons repeated: "This was much easier than I had feared!" or "Man, there are a lot of lonely people out there!" Some wrote, "I thought starting and maintaining the conversations would be the hard part, but the hardest part was getting the heck away from those people!"

No kidding. Do these four things:

1. Make someone feel important.
2. Remember their name.
3. Show interest in their life.
4. Give a sincere compliment.

You will suddenly become the most important person in the lives of others, and they will not want to let you go.

GENEROUSLY TOUCH THE OTHER PERSON

Great conversationalists are quick to extend their hand to shake the hand of friends, old and new. Preachers and ministers grab with both hands. Good friends put their arm around your neck. Close friends feel free to grab you and give you a big bear hug. The best conversationalists in your life are probably the same people most likely to reach out and generously touch you.

Do you know why we shake hands as a social greeting? As a social convention, it could have been anything: bow at the waist, touch foreheads, slap elbows, rub noses, or slap and rub behinds! But no, our culture chose the handshake. Do you know why? As a nonverbal symbol, the handshake says, "I have no weapon, check me out, be at ease, you are safe, and you are O.K.!"

Have you ever shaken someone's hand and immediately formed an unfavorable impression of that person? Most all of us have had that experience. I ask audiences, "What do you call that handshake?" Dishrag, limp wrist, and dead fish are common labels. You shake that hand and can't wait to let go of it, eeeeeyyewwwww! You would think they would know!

How about the complete opposite handshake? Vise grip, gorilla grip, bone-crusher, and macho man are common labels I hear for this handshake. I work with a lot of law enforcement audiences, and I often encounter this handshake. I'll shake hands and say, "Officer, it is a pleasure to meet youuuUUUU! MA'AM! MA'AM!"

MY UNCLE BOB

My Uncle Bob was a bone crusher. When I was a kid, we would go to my grandma's farm in Oklahoma. Most of my mom's family lived close to the farm. Every holiday, I would see plenty of aunts, uncles, and cousins. Inevitably, I would cross paths with my Uncle Bob. "Put 'er there, pal!" he would command, and I would stick my skinny hand into his massive mitt. My Uncle Bob was a big guy. Mama's little brother was probably 240 lbs. at his biggest, and not only would he crush your hand, he would also scrape the bones of your knuckles over one another as he squeezed down hard on your hand. Every time. Every holiday. Curiously, he was my favorite relative. He was a great storyteller, had a terrific and entertaining personality, and was a serious Oklahoma outdoorsman whose parents were both born in Indian Territory.

Every year, I had hoped would be the year I would finally stand up to the "vise grip" only to annually find myself on my knees, begging for mercy, and hollering "UNCLE!"

Decades flew past and visits became regretfully infrequent. One day, I learned my Uncle Bob was diagnosed with stomach cancer. Do you know what they do with those patients? They cut out their stomach and replace it with a plastic bag. Uncle Bob went from a powerful 240 lb. man to a 116 lb. cancer victim about as quick as possible. It looked like the end was near for Uncle Bob, so I went to visit him at the hospital. When I stepped into his room and saw a tiny skeleton of a man lying in the bed, I was sure I was in the wrong room.

I turned to leave when a familiar voice said, "Brian!"

I asked, "Uncle Bob?"

"Of course, get in here," he replied.

I said, "Put it there, pal!" as I grabbed hold of his now skinny and frail hand and started squeezing, HARD. I felt his knuckle bones in his hand grating upon one another as I grinned in delight!

Moral: Be careful how you shake someone's hand; paybacks can be brutal and unexpected.

****

Who Goes First?

I show a slide in my presentations of a gentleman introducing a lady to another man. Who is supposed to extend their hand first, the man or the woman? I find my audiences to be evenly split with the exception of those who say, "Both!" I agree. The modern workplace should be genderless where all are treated the same. Be the first to extend your hand to say, "Be at ease, you are safe, and you are O.K.!"

Have you ever started to shake someone's hand and then thought better of it? You pull it out and then quickly re-holster your hand before anyone notices. For that problem and the problem about who goes first, I offer this advice related specifically to the handshake. I emphasize that this advice applies only to your handshake. You can imagine the look on some young men's faces when I suggest WHEN IN DOUBT, WHUP IT OUT. Be the first to say, "Glad to meet you!"

Also, no matter who you are and no matter who you meet, make certain you shake using your entire hand, look them in the eye, squeeze firmly, and release the moment they relax their grip.

Finally, do not use only your fingertips. Do not squeeze more or less than firm. Do not hang on uncomfortably long for your partner. Finally, do not fail to look your partner in the eye when you shake their hand.

VOLLEY CONVERSATIONS WITH BRIEF COMMENTS AND "RETURN" QUESTIONS

Great conversations resemble a long tennis match. Just as the tennis ball continually crosses from first one side and then to the other, so goes a conversation. Your turn, my turn, your turn, etc. What keeps the conversational volley going are brief comments followed by a question, and then your brief comment followed with a question for your partner.

In my classroom, before I sent students marching out the door, we would have a practice conversation. I picked out the two most different students in the classroom, "You in the back corner, start out by asking your partner on the front row a brief question."

"Wassup?" was a common opening. I would then turn to the student on the front row and, as directed, they would briefly answer the question and then ask a question in return.

The amazing thing about this exercise is that the point is made every time. Two students who appear to have nothing in common find it—every time. Once they find something in common, they begin communicating. The entire classroom learns that when you ask a question, the answer may surprise you! Had one of them not chanced to ask a question, they would have missed a terrific opportunity to learn, once again, what a small world we live in.

The final lesson I gave my students before their march out the door to some fascinating, enlightening, beneficial conversations was The Five Step Proper Introduction:

Stand and smile
Shake their hand
See their eyes
Say your name
Say their name

This strategy also works for those situations in which you see someone across the room and you can't remember their name! With this strategy, you won't have to ask for their name because they should reciprocate your gesture.

CHAPTER FOUR REVIEW:
THE ART OF CONVERSATION

If you can't talk to people who are different than you,
then you are going to have some problems.

Shy people can be great conversationalists because they are
more likely to focus attention on the other person.

Master Conversationalists always make the other person
feel important.

Asking for help is a great way to make someone
feel important.

Everyone is better at remembering faces than names.

Master Conversationalists repeat the other person's name
often in a conversation.

Interesting people are interested people.

Master Conversationalists compliment others easily.

Master Conversationalists generously touch others and are
the first to offer a hand of friendship.

Concerning your handshake: *When in Doubt, Whup it Out!*

Volley your conversations with brief comments and
return questions.

FIVE
The Helping Conversation

While most all of my participants are competent conversationalists, I trust few are trained counselors. However, the few counseling psychologists who have participated have all agreed this lecture includes valuable lessons for anyone seeking to counsel others.

GIVING ADVICE VERSUS GIVING COUNSEL

All of us are experts at giving advice: "Let me tell you what to do; I have all the answers to your problem; just do exactly as I say; listen up and TAKE MY ADVICE."

Counseling goes a little bit like this: "I am not going to tell you what to do, and I assure you I do not have all the answers. I cannot solve your problem for you, but I'll tell you how I can help. I'll sit and listen as you figure out what is best for you to do given your situation. Let me ask you a question…"

DEMONSTRATING EMPATHY

Empathy is not sympathy—two words, two constructs, two different things. Sometimes, we get them confused.

The typical two-word statement of sympathy is ___ _____ .
Repeat after me, if you failed to guess—I'm sorry. That is a two-word statement of sympathy. In seminars, some participants are quick to guess the two words and enthusiastically shout out, "I'M SORRY!"

I often "randomly" pick out a participant and say, "Sir, those words came out of your mouth real quick!"

"Well, I've had a lot of practice!" is the usual reply.

"John, I see you wear a wedding band." I ask, "How long have you been married, and what is your wife's name?"

John replies, "Amy, and we have been married 32 years."

I ask John, "Have the words, 'Amy, I am so sorry' ever crossed your lips?"

He enthusiastically agrees.

I say, "I bet you have said, 'Amy, I am so very sorry. I don't know what else to say other than I'm sorry', on some occasions." He agrees again, accusing me of spying on his household.

I then ask him if he has ever said, "Amy, I am so very sorry. I don't know what else to say other than I'm sorry! I am sorry, I am sorry, I AM SO VERY SORRY! There, now you heard the two words you want to hear: I'm SORRY! Can you get off my back, get over it and drop it? I am sooooo verrrrrrry SORRY!"

Some participants can admit to having had that conversation—last night. They are left bewildered, finally demanding, "What do you want from me? I said I'M SORRY!"

However, I trust few of those in 30 and 40-year marriages have had to admit to that conversation in several decades. They learned, long ago, that the easiest way to deal with difficult people is to give them what they want. Occasionally, what your audience wants is a little empathy.

THE EMPATHIC RESPONSE

Your words demonstrate empathy if they meet these four conditions:
1. They are focused on the other person.
2. They are focused on the other person's feelings, issues, and concerns.
3. They get the other person talking about their feelings, issues, and concerns.
4. They never problem-solve or give advice.

Let's say I am having a conversation with John, and he asks, "How is it going, Brian?"

"O.K., but my Uncle Bob recently died."

"I am sorry," says John.

Let's take a look at this exchange. I share a personal tragedy in my life, and WHO does John focus his words on? WHOSE feelings does he focus his words on?

Does his statement get me talking at all? I would probably weakly say, "Well, thanks." End of conversation. And if not that, I may say, "Oh it's O.K. Don't get upset! We are kind of glad Uncle Bob dropped dead; he tortured me as a kid. In fact, I may have killed him in his hospital bed with my Death Grip! It is O.K."

Don't get me wrong! Statements of sympathy are often appropriate, but they should be followed with some more words. Once again, pull out your most important verbal skill and ask a question: "I'm sorry. Is there anything I can do for you? Were you close to your Uncle? How is his family doing?"

SIMPLE SKILLS ARE RARELY SIMPLE

Demonstrating empathy seems so simple:
Focus your words on your audience!

But simple skills are rarely simple. Let's say someone you know is going through a very difficult point in his or her life. They schedule a session with a counseling psychologist. How much can a respected counselor charge per hour for their professional services?

Most guesses range from $100-$200 per hour. What do they do to earn $150 per hour? They do the following:

1. Focus on the other person.
2. Focus on the other person's feelings, issues, and concerns.
3. Encourage the other person to talk about feelings, issues, and concerns.
4. Never problem-solve or give advice.

Consider just how valuable we could be to the important people in our lives if we could resist the temptation to say: "I AM SO SORRY, BUT WHAT ABOUT ME!"

We find it so hard to find someone in our lives who can expertly dispense a little empathy that we will pay a doctor $150 an hour to do it for us because when something is rare, it is valuable. And when a service is both rare and valuable, it is also expensive.

Below are three principles that guide counselors through these $150 conversations:

1. Acknowledge the opinions and views of others.
2. No one should tell another person what to do.
3. Successful behavior change is self-motivated.

Acknowledge the opinions and views of others. We want so much to be told we are O.K. that we will pay someone $150 an hour to reassure us, to tell us it is O.K. to feel and think the way we do, someone to say, "I will not tell you how to think and feel."

I suppose few of us embrace the second principle: *No one should tell another what to do.* I would also guess not many of us earn $150 per hour for our professional services either. I figure finding people skilled and eager to tell others what to do is probably easy to do. So, we do not have to richly compensate for skills that are not so rare.

But it is difficult to find someone who is dedicated to helping you AND who will not tell you what to do. They are rare people who provide a valuable service—a service we could all do a better job of providing to the most important people in our lives.

Eliminating Misunderstandings

If I am paying someone $150 per hour to counsel me, there sure better not be any misunderstandings. The professional counselor uses a familiar tool we can use to eliminate misunderstandings with our important audiences.

The Tool of Paraphrasing

We can eliminate our misunderstandings by repeatedly asking: "Let me make sure I understand you. What I hear you saying is…" and what follows is only a guess. With confirmation, we proceed with absolute clarity.

If you fail to use this tool in your important conversations, then you will fail to understand your audiences. The primary benefit of paraphrasing:

You get it right the first time!

Through paraphrasing, you eliminate misunderstandings by confirming the meaning of their message. You won't walk away from an important conversation assuming you understand exactly what was meant. You will avoid later revelations that leave you lamenting, "I wish I had asked."

SIX O'CLOCK SHARP

That summer, long ago, when I was presenting a number of two-day communication seminars to the Kenner, Louisiana Police Department, I had an officer approach me with an offer. While I was in town, I was invited to join his running group of fellow police officers who meet every day outside the training facility for training runs along a bike path atop the Mississippi River levee. I enthusiastically accepted the offer to join his group and asked, "What time do we meet back here for our run?"

"Six o'clock. There will be a half-dozen or more runners meeting in the parking lot. We will wait for you, but we try to start at six o'clock sharp. See you there!"

I let class out a little early that day so I would have plenty of time to get to my hotel, make some phone calls, check emails, change clothes, and make it back to the training facility for my group run with the officers that evening.

I drove to the training facility, and I was surprised to find the parking lot completely empty at 5:55 p.m. I got out of my car and waited for five minutes. At 6:00, I began to doubt the officer's sincere promise to wait for me. At 6:05, I climbed the steps leading to the top of the Mississippi River levee and waited another five minutes in the August heat and humidity. As I strained my eyes far down each direction of the path, I saw no one. Stranded, isolated, and already dripping sweat, I slowly began my jog away from the still blistering August sun. Mildly amused at the clever little trick the officers pulled on the professor, I struggled through a 30-minute run completely alone on the levee for every step.

The next day, I stepped into the training room for the second half of the two-day seminar. I was met with a chorus of officers demanding an explanation as to why I stood THEM up for our group run!

I responded, "ME! I waited in the parking lot and up on the levee until I caught on to your little trick!"

Six voices argued, "No way! We waited until 6:15 for you!" Finally, one of the bright ones in our group figured out I had confused 6:00 A.M. and 6:00 P.M.

Then, after realizing I had shown up 12 hours early, the silence was broken by a Cajun accented voice who spoke for the entire group of officers, "Hell Doc, what the hell kinda damn fool is you! Do you not know you is in South Louisiana and it is August! I'll betcha you was the ONLY ignorant sumbitch out there on that ol' levee!"

I raised my hand, once again, wishing I had asked just one more question: "Let me make sure I understand you…"

****

SHUT THEM UP

Not only is paraphrasing a terrific tool to eliminate misunderstanding, it is also a tool to get the occasional audience you want to shut up to actually shut up!

When we want someone to shut up, what do many of us say? Most participants confess: "SHUT UP!" are two words they often use. I ask, "How is that working out for you?" Most then confess, "Not too well."

Try the tool of paraphrasing instead. It works because there is something that sounds even better than *their* words coming out of *their* mouth, and that is the sound of *their* words coming out of YOUR mouth.

No one wants to be misunderstood. If you can get in a word edgewise to interrupt their vociferous diatribe and torrent of words, try, "Let me make sure I understand you. What I hear you saying is…" They will often shut up and listen to their words. You get control of the conversation, not with your words but with their words!

You get them listening, and you have control because you demonstrated empathy. By repeating their words and their story and convinced you truly understand them, they will then be a much more receptive audience to what you have to say.

Why? Because of the Principle of Verbal Reciprocity: *People talk to you the way you talk to them!*

COUNSELING QUESTIONS AND DERA STRUCTURE

The following structure to the counseling session, once again, demonstrates the centrality of active inquiry in our personal and professional lives. You will learn that the same structure that guides a counseling session also applies to organizational strategic planning, important conversations, and efforts at personal growth.

The DERA Structure: *Describe, Explore, Resolve, Action.*

In the counseling session, DERA would work like this:
   Describe your concerns to me.
    (Let me make sure I understand you…)
   Explore: What could one do to address your concern?
    (Paraphrase)
   Resolve: What are you going to do to solve your
    problem?
    (Paraphrase)
   Action: So, the best course of action is for you to…
    (Paraphrase)

Organizations interested in strategic planning for the growth and development of their organizations follow the same DERA Structure. Personal growth and development programs follow the same DERA Structure. And finally, important conversations with our important audiences should follow the same DERA Structure of questions.

Many parents greet their teenage daughters coming home from school with, "How was school?" The most predictable response parents get from teenage girls is, "Fine!" as their daughters disappear once again into the sanctuary of their bedrooms until time for supper.

Not much of a conversation—at supper, try DERA:

Describe: "Tell me the most interesting, disappointing, funny, exciting, infuriating, or heart-warming thing that happened today at school."

Explore: "My, that is a concern. What could you possibly do to improve the situation?"

Resolve: "Sounds to me like you think you should..."

Action: "You do that. I'll be eager to hear how it works!"

The next day, the conversation begins not with, "How's school?" but rather, "Tell me all about how it went with your solution to your concern at school?" I am confident you will get more from your audience than, "Fine!"

SOMETIMES I JUST WANT A LITTLE SYMPATHY

I suggested earlier that occasionally we confuse our audience's need for empathy with a need for sympathy. Sometimes, our audiences actually do want some sympathy. Unfortunately, "I'M SORRY" fails to satisfy most audience's need for sympathy.

Some people are good at giving audiences exactly what they want. Some are skilled at giving a little sympathy when needed.

HARVEY

I love old Jimmy Stewart movies, and one of my favorites is *It's a Wonderful Life*. In that movie, the thesis is the idea that sometimes we say the right thing and are never aware of it; our words and actions, often unknowingly, make important differences in the lives of others. In *It's a Wonderful Life*, an angel shows George Bailey how his words and actions made differences in his entire community. I like that movie because I like holding onto the faith that it might also be true of our words and actions.

But my all-time favorite Jimmy Stewart movie is *Harvey*. In the movie, Stewart plays the character Elwood P. Dowd who has a problem. He can see and talk to an invisible six-foot rabbit named Harvey. This isn't a problem for Elwood, but it is a problem for his family. The family insists Elwood go to a psychiatrist to get cured of his Harvey problem. It was only in my most recent viewing that I realized Harvey only appeared in Elwood's life soon after the death of Elwood's mother. Elwood pleasantly agrees to his family's wishes.

Elwood engages in conversations with the psychiatrist about Harvey and asks the doctor what he wants more than anything else in the world. I recall the doctor sighs and says, "A beautiful woman to hand me a beer as she listens to me talk about all my problems and concerns, and as I talk about all my trials and tribulations, she rubs my head and whispers into my ear, 'You poor thing, you poor, poor thing.'"

Lots of us are starving for a little sympathy, but few of us are as skilled and willing as the beautiful woman in the psychiatrist's dream to give those of us in need exactly what we want.

****

I am a lucky man. My mother was, and my wife is an expert at giving difficult people what they want! Sometimes when I was out on the road, for weeks at a time, traveling and conducting seminars with sometimes less than enthused participants, I would get to feeling a little sorry for myself. When I started feeling the need for a little sympathy, I would just call my mother or Melissa and start whining about all my trials and tribulations of traveling and conducting seminars. First thing I would hear were three words. I ask participants to guess the three words I would hear when hoping for some sympathy. "GET OVER IT!" is often the guess shouted out. "YOU GOT PROBLEMS?" and "WHINY CRY BABY!" are some other guesses I hear frequently.

No, the three words are not those suggested by my participants. And apparently, unlike some, I am a very lucky man. I live with someone who is skilled at saying just the right thing at the right time. My wife and mother shared three pet words to offer anyone hurting for a little sympathy. If you are from the South or have a wonderful Southern woman in your life, you have most certainly heard these three words on several occasions: BLESS YOUR HEART. And they are often followed with, "You poor thing, you poor, poor thing!" And sometimes when I need sympathy, I hear just the right words at the right time. I am a lucky man!

I was recently in Baton Rouge, Louisiana presenting to an audience of almost two hundred (mostly Southern women) at a conference for rape crisis and domestic violence professionals. It turned out the day was both my birthday and my first presentation after the death of my mother the previous week. As I was sharing this lecture, I got to the part where I ask, "What three words do I hear when I am feeling a little sorry for myself?" I then heard, "BLESS YOUR HEART!" shouted out by over one hundred women from Louisiana. They had no idea those three words where just about the best birthday present I could ever receive and were just the right words at the right time!

WHY SO MUCH SYMPATHY?

Why is it so many seem to want so much of our sympathy? Because for some it is a reward!

Who is the biggest complaining malcontent you have to live or work with? Why are they constantly criticizing, condemning, and complaining about every small inconvenience in their pathetic little lives? Why do they do that? Because, eventually, they find an audience to give them what they want, to say to the complainer, "Bless your heart! You poor, poor thing! You don't make enough money to pay all your bills, and your boss is an idiot, and you don't get enough appreciation for all your hard efforts, and no one listens to you! Why, bless your heart, you poor, bitching, complaining malcontent!"

I once had a self-described malcontent in the room holler out, "No one EVER says 'bless your heart' to me!" So, on and on malcontents go until someone gives them what they want.

If the payoff isn't sympathy, it might be what the Roman orator Cicero said thousands of years ago: "The greater the adversity, the greater the glory!" This sentiment has been repeated throughout the centuries by leaders of nations going through adversity.

As a competitive distance runner, I can certainly appreciate: the greater the adversity, the greater the glory. It is one thing to compete in a 5K race (3.1miles), but it is a far more glorious thing to cross the finish line of a marathon (26.2 miles). Why? There are over twenty more miles of adversity to overcome; hence, more personal glory.

Some folks march through life criticizing, condemning, and complaining about the marathon of adversity they have to put up with in their personal and professional lives. Why? If not sympathy, then possibly they are asking for a little glory in the form of a little appreciation, recognition, and reward for all of the adversity they suffer! They march through life, bitching and complaining every step of the way, claiming perceived injustices and entitlement to special privileges!

Malcontents recognize there are rewards in being a victim.

I didn't always work with law enforcement. When cops first became my audience, I was surprised at the number of apparent chronic complainers reportedly working in every police department. Every police chief and police officer could identify a handful of functioning malcontents in their agency. I was surprised these professionals who deal with victims every day of their lives often seek victim status with their words. I mean, if you work in law enforcement and have to convince your audiences you have been victimized, don't your problems pale in comparison to the faces of victims you see each day? Most officers apparently get it, and some regrettably don't.

WHERE WERE YOU SEPTEMBER 11, 2001?

I know where I was. I was in Springfield, Missouri presenting a seminar to 50 judges from Missouri. The seminar began at 8:00 am CST. At 7:50 am, while walking to the seminar room in the hotel where I was staying, I noticed a news story on the TV in the bar of the hotel lobby about an airplane crashing into a World Trade Center Tower minutes before. Focused on the seminar, I marched to the meeting and we began on time.

After an hour, we took a ten-minute break and learned the rest of the story about that airplane and others. We continued the seminar and took breaks every hour to see horror after horror unfold on the TV in the lobby. At lunch, I called my wife and my mother and spoke to each about the morning's events. The seminar continued into the afternoon. As the scheduled ending time approached, I had to apologize to my audience for not covering all of the workbook material. I explained that, unfortunately, due to the day's events and extended breaks, I would not have time to complete the last hour of the planned seminar.

One of the attending judges raised his hand and told me that, during a vote at lunch, the judges all decided to stay in the seminar until they completed all of the material. Well, I believe that was the nicest thing any audience has ever said to me. Needless to say, I was delighted to stay and complete the seminar's final hour.

Years later, I crossed paths with one of those judges in my audience on 9/11. He said, "I wanted to tell you that after your seminar, I saw the movie *Harvey* again. Did you know that in your seminar, you describe your two daughters with the words of Elwood P. Dowd? Watch it again, and you will see what I mean about your description of your daughters!"

Sure enough, early in the movie, Elwood says, "My mother told me a thousand times, you can either be the smartest person in the room or the most pleasant person in the room. When I was young, I was eager to be the smartest in the room, but now I see it serves me best to be the most pleasant one in the room!"

****

Chapter Five Review:
The Helping Conversation

Giving advice is not giving counsel.

Counselors help others come up with their own answers.

Demonstrating empathy is a rare and valuable skill.

Empathic statements:
- ❑ *Focus on the other person.*
- ❑ *Focus on the other person's feelings, issues, and concerns.*
- ❑ *Get the other person talking.*
- ❑ *Never solve problems or give advice.*

Paraphrasing is asking for confirmation, *"Let me make sure I understand you. What I hear you saying is…"*

Paraphrasing allows you to demonstrate empathy and get control of a conversation.

DERA Structure is used in counseling, strategic planning, social conversations, and personal growth:
- ❑ *Describe*
- ❑ *Explore*
- ❑ *Resolve*
- ❑ *Action*

Everyone occasionally wants some sympathy.

Some people want sympathy for the attention and glory.

"Bless your heart, you poor, poor thing" is an effective tool for those seeking to give others some sympathy.

SIX
Errors of Perception

THE FUNDAMENTAL PERCEPTUAL ERROR

I do not see things as they are. I try to constantly remind myself of this fact. Because as soon as I believe I have all the answers, I have just demonstrated how ignorant I really am! The fundamental perceptual error is the belief: *"I see things as they are."*

I don't and you don't, but we like to think we do. Later, we will discuss the psychological comfort of absolute certainty and the discomfort of suggestions otherwise (cognitive dissonance). For now, let us focus on the perception of reality *as we know it*, emphasis on the last four words.

In this chapter, we will examine the subjective reality we must live in and the benefits of communicating provisionally.

SUBJECTIVITY AND PROVISIONAL COMMUNICATION

Each morning, my local newspaper is delivered to my front porch. I retrieve it, and I always start with the sports page. At the bottom of my daily sports page is a 600-word commentary by local columnist and sports editor, Wally Hall. I enjoy the column, and each day I am greeted by his name, his picture, his 600 words, and the title of his daily commentary: *Like It Is.*

Each morning, when I finish reading his 600 words, have I just gotten it LIKE IT IS? Is that an accurate description of what I have just read? Of course not; a more accurate title for the commentary would be something like, AS I SEE IT.

How often do you think his readers feel compelled to tell Wally how wrong he is? But here is the thing about Wally. He loves upsetting folks. He likes for people to write letters, to call his radio and TV talk shows and present a long commentary on how wrong Wally is, and to take the opportunity to let others know just exactly LIKE IT *REALLY* IS. After we read or listen to these insistent voices about how things really are, have we now gotten it LIKE IT IS, or have we been presented with one more version of AS I SEE IT?

If you are like Wally and want to invite conflict, controversy, and irate voices, then enjoy your visit to Wally's World. March in a world of absolute certainty, and I am certain you, too, will get what you ask for. If, perhaps, you wish to reduce the potential conflicts in your life, then communicate *provisionally* and only claim AS I SEE IT, and avoid the fundamental perception error found in Wally's World. With the claim of AS I SEE IT, you allow for provisions that you may be wrong. Absent the finger pointing of absolute certainty, provisionalism is much more acceptable than "let me tell you like it is," even to disagreeing audiences.

Here is how I define perception in my presentations:
The process by which we Select, Organize, and Interpret stimuli to create our own worldview

We have a lot of choice in our worldview. Consequently, we don't see things as they are. We make choices in selection. Everything can't get our full attention. Much of what is going on around us, right in front of us, and behind our back gets ignored. The stimuli that easily captures our attention is that which is vivid and intense. Hence, stop signs are red. Red lights are better, and flashing red lights with noisy sirens blaring are even better. The same principle applies to marketing, public discourse, and interpersonal relations. The louder, more persistent, repetitive, noisy, flashy, bright, colorful, and intense the stimuli, the more likely we are to pay attention.

Perception, Selection, and Relevance

We also are inclined to pay attention to that which is relevant to our own personal egocentric self-interest. That which was particularly attractive to you last year may be of absolutely no interest to you this year. Things that meant nothing to you yesterday now command your attention like nothing else today. Why? One explanation is relevance. Have you ever purchased a car and suddenly noticed exact duplicates of your new car everywhere you drive? Then you experienced relevance in the selection of perceptual stimuli. The world didn't suddenly change on you. Instead, you had a sudden change in how you look at the world.

You See Things as You Are

Just about every demographic that describes you, every experience unique to you, every decision you ever made, and every belief you hold to be true, creates one more filter through which the stimuli that grabs your attention must pass. Since everything can't get through, we filter only that which has relevance to our unique self-interest and unique worldview.

You will perceive the world differently if you are black or white, young or old, eastern or western, Democrat or Republican, carnivore or vegetarian, rich or poor, Christian or Muslim, Texan or New Yorker, tall or short. You will perceive the world uniquely if you are a mixed race middle-aged Midwesterner with average income, medium height, and uncommitted tastes in food who claims independent views on politics and religion. Who you are shapes what you pay attention to. And on that limited and selective input, you form your worldview of the way things are.

Police officers and prosecutors all know that eyewitness testimony is one of the weakest forms of evidence one can bring to the courtroom. Everyone uniquely selects and interprets events leading to conflicting eyewitness sworn testimony. Divorce courts, custody hearings, and civil lawsuits are probably good places to find examples of how self-interest and best intentions can shape entirely different perceptions of the same events.

A common graphic used to illustrate how we select, organize, and interpret stimuli is the one below.

When I was speaking to the South Carolina Sheriff's Association, I showed the graphic above and asked, "Sheriffs, what do you see?"

A heavy set good ol' boy of a Sheriff seated in the back proclaimed, "I see mah mother-in-law!"

I turned and said, "Well then…your mother-in-law must be a young, attractive woman like the one I see in the picture!"

"Oh no," he said. "My mother-in-law looks just like the witch I see up there. I call her 'Sea-Hag'!"

Once that Sheriff locked onto the organization and interpretation of the picture depicting an old woman, he could not re-organize and re-interpret the image to see the slight profile of a young attractive woman. Even with the insistent and increasingly frustrated urgings and efforts of his colleagues, the Sheriff could not see things another way.

Interestingly, I understand that the picture above first appeared in *The New Yorker* magazine in 1905 and was titled "My Wife and My Mother-in-Law."

Here is one I bet you haven't seen. Look below and determine what you see.

If you are like most folks, you can see both a woman's face and a guy playing a saxophone. The woman's face is more difficult to see because you have to make the image three-dimensional with the dark in the background and the white in the foreground to create the dark shadow of a face.

If you are like some folks, you looked at the previous image and didn't see just any guy playing a saxophone. In fact, in Arkansas just about everyone sees the same particular guy: Former President Bill Clinton.

Look at the next image and determine which of the two circles in the middle is the bigger circle, the one surrounded by other circles on the left or the one on the right?

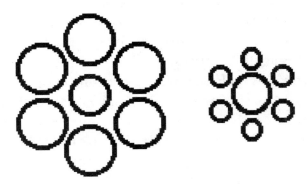

You may be surprised to learn that the two are exactly the same size. The one on the right only looks bigger because of what surrounds it. This is why your mother said, "Choose your friends carefully. People judge you by your surroundings." The graphic also demonstrates that those who may have recently gained a bunch of weight may want to get rid of their old skinny friends and find a new group of truly obese friends to include in their circle. They will then be seen as the skinny one in their group!

Look closely at the image of an elephant:

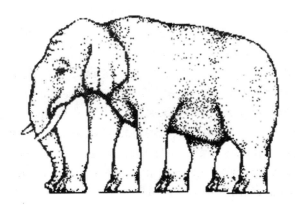

Looking at this image may kind of hurt your head. This feeling is called Cognitive Dissonance. The term, coined by social psychologist Leon Festinger, translates to mean "unpleasant thoughts." The elephant is hurting your head because the image causes Cognitive Dissonance. The image is unpleasant to our cognitive thought processes because we prefer certainty and closure, and this image provides us with neither. We franticly count the elephant's legs and study the edges to find something in the image that will provide relief. There is none. So, we turn away from the image and find relief only by avoiding the image.

Cognitive Dissonance has a profound impact on our selection and interpretation of the information we encounter and events we observe. We like to be right. There is comfort in being certain you have all the answers and see things exactly as they are. We like to think of ourselves as motivated by the greater good of all, as intelligent and important people worthy of appreciation.

We do not like the suggestion that we are wrong, stupid, unimportant, or unworthy of respect. In fact, I believe the most common way you experience cognitive dissonance is when someone steps up and tells you that you are not O.K. That suggestion creates cognitive dissonance. That is an unpleasant thought, so we actively avoid that which causes cognitive dissonance. Therefore, if you are the type of person who delights in pointing out all of the ways that people are not O.K., then I predict people are actively avoiding you, avoiding your calls, and avoiding time spent with the source of so much cognitive dissonance.

We also avoid groups, literature, books, articles, websites, and audiences that might suggest we are not perfect in every way! We seek confirmation of our beliefs, values, behavior, decisions, and worldview as the one correct ideology for all. We find comfort in the familiar, the consistent, and the predictable. We desire consensus and agreement, and we avoid any suggestion that we may be slightly mistaken.

We are often, perhaps usually, slightly mistaken. Perhaps we need a slap in the head, a change in perspective, a new outlook, a heightened awareness, and a reminder that maybe we aren't perfect in every way. Occasionally, our perceptions need to be confronted.

But we do not want to hear that we are not O.K. So, we cover our ears, close our eyes, and focus our attention elsewhere, someplace where the environment is free of cognitive dissonance. We avoid, avoid, and avoid. We select, organize, and interpret events to support our worldview.

We will return to the consequences of cognitive dissonance later. But for now, just remember we don't like it and we avoid it.

We Do Not Like to be Wrong

Take a look at the line below that is divided into two segments, Segment "A" and Segment "B". Without actually measuring the lengths, tell me which segment is longer, "A" or "B"?

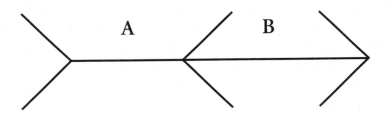

Most participants say, "They are the same." If you also said, "They are the same; neither A or B is longer," then I say congratulations to you. That is the answer most experienced participants give. However, if I ask which segment looks longer, most will agree B *looks* longer. But again, most still say "A" and "B" are the same length in spite of appearances.

Expectations Guide Your Perceptions

Sometimes, we see and hear just exactly what we expect to see and hear. We select, interpret, and organize events to fit into our predetermined expectations. After some major and unexpected event, my mother would often proclaim that she knew beforehand that it was going to happen. She could now recall a dream the previous week that forecasted the event. If not a dream, she was certain she had just been silently worrying that such a thing might happen soon to the unfortunate victim.

Let's take a test. Answer with the first thing that pops into your head. Ready!

Question One: A punch line comes at the end of a _____.

Question Two: From a tiny acorn grows a mighty _____.

Question Three: The part of an egg that is white is called the _____.

If your answer to Question Three was yolk, please re-read the question. The white part of an egg, I believe, is called the albumen or simply the egg white.

Why do so many say YOLK? Because they *expected* the answer to rhyme with JOKE and OAK. Those clever folks think they have figured out the pattern. In fact, that is what our brains help us do, detect the pattern. Once we have identified the pattern of events, we have the comfort of prediction and control. Our faith in the certainty of the pattern provides the confidence to shout out the complete wrong answer about the white of the egg.

Sometimes We See and Hear What We Expect

Go back and look at the line split into Segment A and Segment B, and tell me now which segment is longer.

Some still insist the segments are the same length. A lot of folks now confidently say, "B". Most are not nearly as sure as they were a minute ago when they were certain B only *looks* longer.

In reality, B looks longer because it *IS* longer. Because experienced participants have an expectation that the answer is always "They are the same," they are certain A and B are the same although B looks longer.

Sometimes, our experience misinforms us by giving false assurances that things are the same. We have seen it before, maybe dozens of times. It is the same; they are the same; the outcome is the same; the cause is the same. "It is the same thing," we confidently proclaim secure in the certainty that we have discovered the secret and that we can see things as they really are!

If you just have to measure, go now and determine for yourself that B actually is longer.

Welcome back. Take a look at the two tables below. You may see a long skinny table and a short wide table.

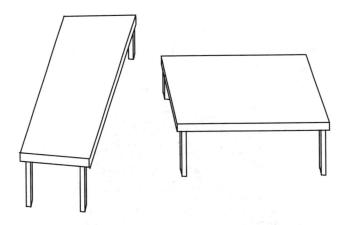

If you see two tables of different dimensions along the tabletop, you are mistaken. The two tabletops have the exact same dimensions: same length and same width. The tabletops are the same. They don't look the same but they are. How about that!

Lots of participants are still sure they are NOT the same and are convinced my claim that the tabletops are the same is most certainly wrong.

I ask, "Who is 100% certain the tabletops are NOT the same?" Lots of confident hands appear.

To prove the tabletops equal, I take an exact paper copy of the long skinny tabletop. I place it over the long skinny table top on an overhead transparency to demonstrate that the paper cutout and the long, skinny tabletop are exactly the same size and shape. I then drag the paper cutout and cover the other table, exactly.

Those in the room who previously had their 100% certain hands in the air are saying to themselves, "Dang, I wish I had said I was only 99% certain and that they only LOOK different to me!" But they took a trip to Wally's World and told themselves I see things AS THEY ARE.

Can You See Jesus?

Focus your eyes on the image below. Stare at the image for 30 seconds. Then close your eyes and study the inside of your eyelids for a few seconds. Wait for a circle to appear. Be patient.

It's Right in Front of Your Eyes

My young daughter seemed delighted to share the next one with me. She got an email that instructed her to **count the number of times the letter F is used below:**

FINISHED FILES ARE THE RE-
SULT OF YEARS OF SCIENTIF-
IC STUDY COMBINED WITH THE
EXPERIENCE OF YEARS

If you are like me, the first time you tried, you came up with only three. You are wrong. Actually, there are six. Try again to find all six.

Lots of folks are like that South Carolina Sheriff. Once you see things one way, it is difficult to see it in another way. If you can still see only three letter Fs in the text, refocus on the words just before and after the word YEARS.

And you want to claim you see things as they are when many of you can't see the six Fs even when they are right in front of your eyes. Interestingly, this demonstrates that as we read we listen to our words, and if the F doesn't sound like an F, as in OF, then we don't see the F.

WE DON'T SEE THINGS AS THEY ARE

The perceptual exercises demonstrate that we are not all that accurate in how we view the world through the process of selecting, organizing, and interpreting stimuli. Sometimes, things that *are* the same do not *look* the same. Other times, things we are certain *look* the same *are not* the same. We seek consensus and avoid cognitive dissonance. We are attracted to novelty and overlook the mundane. Sometimes, we see things that are not there, and other times we can't see what is right in front of our eyes.

I intend to create some doubt in your ability to see things as they are. If I am successful, you will be more willing to ask questions and communicate provisionally. You will reduce the times you look or sound stupid and avoid falling victim to the fundamental perceptual error.

Now Try This

Reecnt stdueis indcitae taht eevn wehn wrods r miseplled, fi the frist & lsat ltrs r n teh cerrcet pstions, u kann raed the sintnece and xtrcat tehe corerct menagin. Tihs is bcuseae the hmaun mnid deos not raed ervey lteter by istlef, but hte wrod as a wlohe. Pertty naet!

This exercise demonstrates that we are capable of organizing stimuli, interpreting patterns, and seeing things as they are. With enough clues, we can figure out exactly what is going on; however, not as often as we wish and believe.

Errors of Attribution

Have you ever asked yourself, "Why did they do that?" or "Why did I do that?" Your answer is your attribution. You attribute the cause of that behavior to this explanation. You just created an explanatory hypothesis seeking to attribute causal forces to observed or reported activities. You identified the pattern, if A then B; therefore, if B then A.

Your attribution will be one of two types: Internal or External.

An Internal Attribution suggests that behavior is the result of internal characteristics and motives. The attribution is that only certain types of people do that type of behavior: heroic, intelligent, honest, altruistic, moral, responsible, foresighted, persistent, talented, self-motivated,

or

irresponsible, selfish, stupid, evil, vindictive, unethical, cowardly, deceptive, immoral, greedy, or any of a thousand possible internal characteristics and motives. "Why was the victim brutally murdered?" the prosecutor asks the jury. "Because the defendant is a cold-blooded murderer out for revenge!"

An External Attribution suggests they did that behavior because of circumstance, luck, destiny, and any of a thousand possible external explanations: the environment, his schooling, the hand of God, "the Devil made me do it," bad timing, perfect timing, the whites, the blacks, the Christians, the Jews, the butler did it. "Why did my client kill the alleged 'victim'?" the defense attorney asks the jury. "Because my client was merely acting in self-defense!"

I would ask my students to imagine that already this morning they had observed the following:

A man beating a dog with a stick
  (as you drove your dog to the vet)
A woman speeding through a red light
  (at an intersection where you were stopped)
A fellow student receive a failing grade
  (on a test that you got an A on)
Another student get caught cheating on an exam
  (a behavior you would never do)
Yet another student talking rudely to an instructor
  (your favorite teacher)

You ask yourself, "Why are that man, that woman, and those students doing those things?" You make attributions:

"That man is an animal abuser!"
"That woman is a law-breaker!"
"That student is stupid, that one is a cheater, and that one is just plain rude!"

INTERNAL BIAS IN ATTRIBUTIONS OF OTHERS

Each of your attributions are based on your experience, your perspective, your judgment, and your perceptions. We have already demonstrated the problems associated with the selection, organization, and interpretation of stimuli.

Let's do a role reversal. Let us now say I catch you beating your dog, breaking traffic laws, failing an exam, cheating on an exam, and talking rudely to your teacher.

I ask you, "Why did you do that?"

How many would answer the question with:

"I am an animal abusing, traffic violating lawbreaker who is stupid, unethical, and rude."

Not likely. You are going to see things a bit differently. You will find an external attribution to justify the behavior.

"That dog was attacking me!"

"The light was yellow, and you are a racist!"

My failing student could explain to his mother, "I failed the exam because I am stupid, Mama. It is probably a hereditary condition." Notice the claim begins as internal and concludes with an external attribution for his stupidity!

Personal responsibility was rarely the attribution of my former students for their failed exams. My students usually found someone else to blame for their failures: their professor! He is the one with tricky questions, misleading lectures, and evil intentions.

External attributions are often "useful lies" that free us from personal accountability. "Why was I talking rudely? It's his fault; he started it. I was talking to him just like he was talking to me. It's all his fault!"

Self-Serving Bias in Personal Attributions

We do not necessarily favor external attributions for our successes but rather only for our failures. Who do we see as the person responsible for our successes? Ourselves, of course!

Let's say the former failing student turns his grade around to an A+ on the next exam. The student rushes home and proclaims, "Look what I did; I got an A!" Mama asks, "Why success now?" He explains, "My professor gave an easy exam that any idiot could pass!" Not likely.

He most likely would explain, "I earned it; I'm smart; I am responsible for my successes." Others are accountable for his failures.

The self-serving bias will guide our perceptions to determine which attribution will best serve our self-interest.

Cognitive Dissonance

Earlier, you looked at the graphic of an elephant, and we defined cognitive dissonance as the uncomfortable feeling associated with viewing the graphic.

I also suggested the most common way we both cause and experience cognitive dissonance is when we tell someone or are told, "You are not O.K."

We do not like dissonance and will actively take steps to reduce the unpleasantness. Festinger suggests that there is a hierarchy of five strategies available to us in our efforts to cope with the dissonance associated with being told, "You are not O.K."

Avoidance

Predictably, we avoid the source of this unpleasantness, just as we turned our eyes away from the elephant.

Recently, I was at a party when a friend began a graphic description of her bloody and infected tooth that was forcibly and painfully extracted by her dentist. I quickly extracted myself from the unpleasant conversation and desperately searched for another partygoer to visit with!

If the source of your unpleasantness is unavoidable (parent, spouse, boss, colleague, child), you are going to have to come up with a new strategy to cope with your cognitive dissonance.

Imagine a hopelessly addicted cigarette smoker sitting in his favorite chair at home watching his favorite television program. He reaches for a new pack of his favorite brand of cigarettes from a recently purchased carton.

Everything is O.K. Then his favorite program is interrupted by a public service announcement from the American Cancer Society. The message is going to suggest the smoker is not O.K. He is not healthy; he is not too smart; he is not looking out for the best interest of the people he lives with. The PSA is produced and broadcast at considerable effort and expense for this very audience: the smoker! But how much of that 60-second message suggesting the intended audience is not O.K. is the smoker going to watch?

I guess about three seconds—just enough time to locate, secure, and use the remote control to change the channel to something else, anything else!

Now, let's say the message is on every channel at the same time. He turns the TV off. In every room he steps into, he finds someone demanding that he stop, quit now, and just say no!

Avoiding the dissonance isn't possible, and a new coping strategy needs to be found and employed.

In fact, there is a predictable hierarchy of strategies for coping with cognitive dissonance. First, we avoid.

When that isn't possible, we do what the smoker often does when he proclaims: "Well, no kidding, smoking is going to kill me. I know I'll probably die from it. But you know, everyone is going to die, and I'd rather die happy with a cigarette in my hand than quit and live frustrated and unhappy. I've tried to quit before, and it isn't a pretty sight. I get grumpy, irritable, and I say regrettable things to important people. Look, in the interest of world peace, it is best I keep killing myself!"

RATIONALIZATION

Reducing the importance of the change is the second likely strategy. "Oh sure, that is important, but this is even more important. It is really not that big a deal. You are making a mountain out of a molehill. I do good with this and this, so get off my back about that."

If this strategy of rationalization fails to convince your audience the change isn't that important, you will need a new strategy. Next, we look at the third strategy for coping with cognitive dissonance.

But first, here is a question for you:

What is the one thing that is better than actually being O.K.?

ANSWER: Having others THINK that you are O.K.

See, you may actually be O.K. (doing the right thing). But if you get blamed for someone else's mistake (your audience thinks you are not O.K.), you are definitely not O.K. with that.

However, if you are actually NOT O.K. (doing the wrong thing) and your audience THINKS you are O.K. (doing the right thing), you are probably O.K. with that!

So, we are egocentrically motivated to conceal our flaws, put on our best face, convince our audiences that we are really doing the right thing even, perhaps especially, when we are actually doing the wrong thing.

ARGUMENTATION

Argumentation and debate allow me to attempt to convince you I really am O.K. This third strategy can also involve active avoidance of discussions about the behavior deemed NOT O.K.! Engagement or avoidance, the goal is the same: convince you I am O.K. so you can't tell me that I am not.

So begins extensive efforts of explanation, justification, omissions, white lies, self-deception, posing, acting, hiding, pretending, distorting, manipulating, gate-keeping, and defending your goal of being told you are O.K.

Perhaps less effort would go into actually doing the right thing, but many of us appear before our audiences, performing on stage, and delivering all the right words in just the right way. After the performance for our critics and the spotlight is off and the curtain is down, we actors go out the backstage door into the darkness and go about doing things our way, the wrong way.

Students of communication are particularly interested in two areas related to this discussion: vocabulary and persuasion. Both are linked to image formation and identity. No one wants to look stupid and everyone wants to be seen as O.K. So, students are often eager to expand their vocabulary and skills of persuasion.

If your persuasive arguments that "I am O.K." fail, you need a new coping strategy. Let's review the material so far. The most common way we experience cognitive dissonance is when we are told we are not O.K. and need to change. When it happens, we AVOID the source. Then, if necessary, we reduce the importance through RATIONALIZATION. If those strategies do not work, we attempt to change the dissonant opinion often through active ARGUMENTATION.

The above reminds us of the difficult job of police, supervisors, and parents. These roles demand that we occasionally have to remind others their behavior is not O.K. Your audiences do not want to hear it. They do all they can to avoid getting caught. They argue that you are being unreasonable in your demands, and they do all they can to convince you that they really are O.K. through varying means of manipulation.

Now, if your audience still insists you are not O.K., then you need a new strategy.

PERSONAL ATTACK

I often stop my seminars at this point and ask one of my participants directly, "How am I doing today?" The selection of whom to query is never random. The first answer is almost always a less than enthusiastic, "O.K." I ask another participant, and they sigh and say, "Fine." I go to another, another, and another. They shrug and say, "All right, I guess." "Not bad," and "o.k."

I then pick the one participant I know will give me the answer I want and ask, "How am I doing?" They grin and say, "Absolutely GREAT! You are the best instructor I have ever had, and you are doing FANTASTIC!" I am then absolutely delighted to declare this student My Favorite Student and enthusiastically present them with an engraved trophy recognizing them as such.

Finally, I turn to the class and ask, "What if instead, she had answered, 'Polansky, you suck! You are a four-eyed, pencil-necked, know-it-all, cocky, arrogant jerk!'"

What are the chances I would have said, "You are still my favorite student! Thank you so much for your honesty. Here, have a nice trophy!"

Not very likely. One of the toughest burdens of a Christian philosophy is that practitioners are supposed to "love your enemy." That is difficult. Because as soon as you tell me I am wrong, I need to change, and I am not O.K., well then, "You are not O.K. You are not my friend any more. You hate me so I hate you! How dare you suggest that I am NOT O.K. Let me tell you just exactly how NOT O.K. you are, and your mother, and your whole stupid family!"

That is the next to last strategy for coping with the dissonance. They are O.K. as long as they tell me I am O.K., but as soon as they suggest I am not perfect in every way, well, then they are definitely NOT O.K.!

This theory is an example of a Balance Theory. We do what we can to balance pain and pleasure. I'm O.K., you're O.K. is balanced. I'm not O.K., you're O.K. is unbalanced. One way to balance things out is to claim, "If I'm not O.K., then you're NOT O.K.!" Balanced.

No wonder many of us prefer to see the police as bullies, our parents as clueless, and our supervisors as idiots! For those who have problems with authority figures, seeing your boss as an idiot is comforting, and the perception is a dissonance coping tool. Because when he says, "You are NOT O.K.!", it is O.K. with you because he is an idiot.

One more quick observation: Remember when I told you the first person I ask in my seminars, "How am I doing today?" always answers with a less than enthusiastic, "o.k."? That person is never random. We have been together for several hours, and we have covered much of the material in this book up to this point. Sometimes, I am forced to continue to ask, and ask, and ask a dozen or more participants before one of them finally, reluctantly, gives me the answer I want, "GREAT!"

I use their reluctance to demonstrate the common principle of dealing with difficult people: GIVE THEM WHAT THEY WANT!

I also occasionally have used the opportunity to ask these reluctant participants to look deep inside themselves to answer WHY they were so reluctant, even if they didn't believe it was true, to tell their professor the one thing they had to know he was going to keep asking, and asking, and asking for? Why couldn't they tell him what he wanted to hear? Why not?

What is the last thing the nicotine addict is going to do to stop all the chronic avoidant behavior, to stop the ongoing rationalization, manipulation, and confrontation? What is the last thing any of us do to end the cognitive dissonance associated with the certainty that we may be wrong and need to change our behavior?

CHANGE

The last thing is often the right thing. But change is hard. Change takes effort and time. Change often takes a little help.

What is the last thing the counseling psychologist says to his clients? "I'll see you next week!"

Unfortunately, our audiences are usually not willing to wait weeks for us to change. They all want us to change instantly. Our bosses drag us into their office and proclaim "STOP THAT NOW. I demand immediate change!"

And we say to ourselves, "Idiot."

CHAPTER SIX REVIEW:
ERRORS OF PERCEPTION

The Fundamental Perceptual Error is the belief:
I see things as they are.

Perception was defined as:
the process by which we Select, Organize, and Interpret stimuli to create our own worldview.

Communicating provisionally acknowledges we may be mistaken in our perceptions.

We don't see the world as it is; we see the world as we are.

We tend to attribute internal explanations for the behavior of others.

We tend to be self-serving in our attributions of our own behavior by taking personal responsibility for our successes and blaming others for our failures.

Cognitive Dissonance can be roughly translated to mean *unpleasant thoughts.*

The most common way we experience cognitive dissonance is when we are told, *"You are not O.K."*

Coping strategies for Cognitive Dissonance:
- ❑ Avoidance
- ❑ Rationalization
- ❑ Argumentation
- ❑ Personal Attack

The final strategy for coping with cognitive dissonance is to actually change.

SEVEN
Conflict Management

If you march through life constantly reminding the most important people in your life that they are NOT O.K., expect a significant amount of conflict in your life. If your roles in life require that you "police behavior," you better be skilled in conflict management!

This chapter summarizes the critical content of a conflict management course I taught at the University. Here is a brief definition I used in the classroom.

Conflict: the expressed struggle between parties who *perceive* **incompatible goals, values, and beliefs.**

I argue that conflict management is best viewed as *perception* management. When we focus on the perception of incompatibility as the problem, the conflict management solution is obvious: help the other party perceive your goals, values, and beliefs as being compatible with theirs.

THE VILLA INCIDENT

Years ago, I taught a summer school class at the University that concluded just before the lunch hour. One August day, in the minutes before I was to dismiss my students, I could hear my colleagues conversing about their immediate lunch plans. I gathered from the conversation in the hallway that my colleagues were going to The Villa Restaurant a couple of miles north of campus on the appropriately named University Avenue.

The Villa was a small but popular lunch spot for the campus crowd, and the restaurant had very limited seating and parking. By noon, there was usually quite a line of folks waiting to get a seat, and if you weren't seated by 11:59, you were not going to be seated for quite some time.

It sounded like almost all of my colleagues were gathering to go without me. As I rapidly concluded the class with a review for the next quiz, students started asking lots of specific review questions.

Now, I love The Villa, and they make this dish called Villa Fettuccini. It is made with spinach noodles, Alfredo sauce, lots of parmesan, artichoke hearts, and large shrimp. It was now 11:49, and students were still peppering me with questions, but all I could think about was The Villa and the clock.

I am also the kind of person who hates to be left behind. I could hear the crowd of delighted colleagues rushing down the hall to beat the lunch rush at The Villa, and my heart sank. I was feeling a little sorry for myself. "Poor, poor me," I silently sighed to myself. "My friends left me behind, hungry and alone." I pouted and then frowned to myself, "I don't want to go with them anyways. They are NOT...!"

Just then, my good friend and colleague, Gary, interrupted my students to say, "We are all going to The Villa. Do you want me to save you a place at the table?"

I gratefully accepted, "Absolutely, Gary. Save me a place at the table!"

After class, even more student questions slowed my exit from the classroom. After a rapid litany of "You're O.K., that will be O.K., and you are going to be O.K.," I raced to my car to begin the two-mile drive from campus to The Villa. I zoomed through a now crowded and busy University Avenue (a major six-lane North/South thoroughfare). Driving north, I glanced at my watch, 12:07. Moments later, I finally saw The Villa on the opposite west side of the road. I saw folks already lined up outside the front door. I also spied absolutely no parking spots at the restaurant.

However, on the east side of the road, less than 100 yards further north, I saw a pest control business with a small but almost empty eight-car parking lot. I thought to myself, "Surely no one would mind if I park there, scramble on foot across six lanes of busy traffic, eat lunch with my colleagues, and then get back and out of the lot before 1:00 pm!" In the time it took me to think that thought, I was parked in a spot.

I quickly exited my car and tiptoed to the curb for my six-lane crossing of University to get to The Villa. I successfully "froggered" my way across the first three lanes of northbound traffic and caught my breath while pausing in the median. As I stood studying the southbound traffic zipping by, inches in front of my nose, I anxiously awaited the next opportunity to complete my journey across University Avenue. Then, just barely above the cacophony of lunch hour summer traffic, I heard a faint voice coming from behind me, "Hey you, hey you…Hey YOU!"

Then the opening in the southbound traffic I had been waiting for appeared. I ran due west away from the voice and across my final three lanes of traffic arriving safely in the strip mall parking lot 70 yards away from the front door of The Villa. I took an immediate left and focused my attention on my luncheon destination. Being goal oriented, I ignored the distant voice now yelling, "HEY YOU…WHAT IS YOUR PROBLEM…HEYYYYY!"

I took a few quick steps and heard, "HEY YOU, YOU STUPID IDIOT, STOP!" and I stopped. "You know sometimes," I said to myself, "I answer to that. I wonder if that gentleman is referring to me?" I took a quick glance across the six lanes of traffic into the pest control parking lot, and I saw a visibly angry and red-faced pest control professional pointing his finger directly at me. Before we could make eye contact, an entire convoy of 20 or more Wal-Mart tractor-trailers filled all three of the northbound lanes between the two of us. I was less than 200 feet from the safety of The Villa's front door and took off walking in the hope that I could quickly disappear inside.

I could hear the man, now screaming expletives by the dozen, shouting at me through six lanes of traffic. I looked ahead and saw, getting out of his car in the last Villa parking spot, my colleague Gary.

He paused his progress to the front door in an effort to figure out exactly what was going on with all the cussing across the street, and then he saw me racing toward him.

I took another glance back over my shoulder and saw the now even angrier pest control professional had just made it through the Wal-Mart convoy and was quickly stepping off the median into the final three clear lanes of University Avenue.

I picked up my pace in the final yards and jogged up to Gary with a look of panic etched onto my face. Gary was looking past me at the enraged gentleman rushing up to us. We all converged at the same time. I could feel my pursuer's breath on the back of my neck as he screamed, "WHAT THE HELL IS YOUR PROBLEM, YOU STUPID IDIOT?"

Gary poked me and said, "I think he is talking to you."

I turned and got my first look at this guy. He was a red-faced, muscle-bound, tattooed, red-headed angry man with fists clenched. I saw thick veins bulging from his forehead, neck muscles straining, and murderous blue eyes boring a hole right through me. I turned to him and said these words, "You are going to have to talk slower, I can't understand you."

But what he heard were those words delivered with the tone, pronunciation, and articulation of an obviously deaf person:

"OU ARRAH GOWING TO HAD TO AUK SLOWAH."

I continued, "I am deaf; you must slow down," with the same labored tongue.

I am NOT proud of this story, but I am proud of the fact no man has ever hit me. Ever! To keep that record going, I have, on occasion, done things others might never dream of doing, like pretending to be deaf.

However, based on his reaction, you would have thought I hit him hard in the face with a two-by-four. His head snapped back and his eyes widened with a confused look. The gentleman stepped back, moved his hands as if steering the wheel of a car, took a deep breath, and very slowly shouted, "YOUUUUU ARE GOING TO HAVVVVVE TO MOOOOVE YOUR CAR!"

I interrupted him and asked, "Moo? Cow?" as I mimicked his hand motions to represent milking a cow. By now, Gary has disappeared into The Villa with our colleagues.

The gentleman took another deep breath and said, "Have a nice day!" He then turned and sprinted through six lanes of traffic and into the pest control business slamming the door behind him.

****

Once again, I am not proud of that story. But it is a great story to illustrate that conflict management is perception management. *The Villa Story* also demonstrates that sometimes it is not what you say but rather HOW you say it!

Psychological Emergencies

You know you are in an emergency if the situation meets these two criteria:

1. The outcome is important
2. The outcome is uncertain

Thousands of potential situations fit these conditions. The more important and the more uncertain the outcome, the bigger the emergency you have to cope with. If someone threatens your life, then you correctly assess the situation as an emergency.

Law enforcement officers are constantly placed in threatening situations where the outcome is both critical and very uncertain. College students taking an important exam to their futures, going on a date with an attractive person for the first time, giving a speech the first day of class, or getting pulled over by a police officer—each situation is one that qualifies perceptually as an emergency.

PHYSIOLOGICAL RESPONSE

Once we cognitively assess the situation as an emergency, our bodies automatically respond to prepare us to physically meet the emergency.

We call that response Fight or Flight. The response is a part of our genetic heritage as a mammal on this planet. All mammals have this important survival response or they wouldn't survive. Our caveman ancestors needed to have a rapid and appropriate response if the bears came back to reclaim the cave. The caveman's two appropriate responses were fight or flight—pick up a weapon and defend his ground or drop everything and take flight.

Today, when we perceive a threat, the adrenalin stored just for these occasions gets deposited into our bloodstream. The brain commands the heart to pump harder to quickly distribute the adrenalin to the arms and legs where the oxygen and adrenalin can be used to stand and fight or to take flight from our conflicts. Engage or retreat. Either way, you had better start your heart to pumping.

This response serves all of God's good creatures in the jungle. Fight or flight or be lunch! I am told 80% of all vertebrate species on this planet have wings. Only birds typically get to be brightly colored red, blue, orange, or yellow. Because when a colorful bird attracts attention and is threatened by a jungle cat, birds can take wing and rise above the conflict.

The other 20% are stuck on terra firma. Those species without wings often have no choice but to fight their way through their conflicts. So, they grow big teeth, big jaws, big claws, and their color blends with the environment. Other species grow huge with thick skins and big horns so they can do a better job of fighting through potential conflicts. Still other species of mammals grow big eyes, big ears, and fast feet so they, like their winged neighbors above, can anticipate, avoid, and take flight from potential emergencies.

The Villa Story illustrates Fight or Flight reactions in humans. Some of us, when faced with a conflict, are quick to take flight; others of us are determined to fight our way through conflict. Those of us with wings or quick feet are often quick to take flight; those of us without wings are often inclined and prepared to fight through conflict. It is human nature.

PITY THE POOR PUBLIC SPEAKING STUDENT

Imagine a college student who REALLY prefers not to look stupid. Because of degree requirements, the student must attend an introductory public speaking class. One day, the student arrives to class to deliver her first speech. The student wishes she had taken more time to prepare because the grade today is a major part of the final course grade. The student takes a seat and sees other speakers confidently step to the front of class and expertly deliver obviously well prepared presentations with poise and good humor.

The student assesses this situation as one in which the outcome is both important and uncertain. That student cognitively concludes that THIS IS AN EMERGENCY!

Her body responds by pumping adrenalin into her bloodstream. Her digestion shuts down in the perceived emergency causing her mouth to go dry and her breakfast to sit uncomfortably in her queasy, butterfly-filled stomach.

Her pounding heart flushes her face red, and the physical excitement of the rush of adrenalin is making the room hot, real hot! The tiny muscles in her face, eager to do something, start occasionally twitching uncontrollably. She thinks, "Man, this room is really hot," as sweat stains her shirt, and she wipes her brow.

She awkwardly stands to present her speech. Her instructor is hoping for a comfortable, confident speaker, but every fiber of that unprepared student's body wants to keep walking out the door and take flight to anywhere there isn't an audience.

As an instructor, I often had many uncomfortable and less than confident students appear in my office just before class—students with pounding hearts, trembling voices, sweaty bodies, and flushed faces eager to be anywhere but in front of an audience. "Help me," they would plead. "Help me get rid of these reactions that torment me every time I have to give a speech!"

"Then I'll have to kill you," I would explain to my pleading students. "These reactions are normal, expected, and beneficial when an outcome is important and unknown."

Over the years, I began anticipating these conversations. The common causes of stage fright appeared to be a combination of the fear of looking stupid, unreasonable expectations of perfection, over-estimations of unimportant factors, and most often, the uncertainty of performance.

That is why, early in the semester, I would address these issues repeatedly. We would talk about the consequences of the fear of looking stupid. Remember, the rare students who claim to have no fear of looking stupid are the same ones who can confidently present even an impromptu presentation before a large audience.

I would remind my students that it is O.K. to occasionally stumble over a pronunciation or briefly lose your place. It is O.K. because no one expects you to be perfect, and 90% still gets you an "A" in my class.

The most important advice I give to any student of effective communication, in any context, is to BE PREPARED. Reduce all uncertainty through rehearsal and revision. Know your opening, your main points, your transitions, and your support. Construct a logically organized outline, and be so familiar with the content that you need only a minimum of notes. Be certain of how long the speech takes you to present, and know exactly how you will summarize and conclude.

COPING WITH SPEECH ANXIETY

Six quick tips for coping with the anxiety of Fight or Flight associated with stage fright:
1. Be prepared with a planned outline of thoughts.
2. Focus on what is most important
   (your audience, not your image).
3. Know your message.
4. Emphasize how your message will help.
5. Adapt to your particular audience.
6. Imagine how a confident and comfortable version of
   you would talk to this audience, and ACT like that!

THE MOST IMPORTANT SPEECHES OF OUR LIFE

This chapter is on conflict management, not public speaking. However, both involve managing the perceptions of your audience. Both require managing the physical reactions of Fight or Flight. Both demand the right words said at the right time in the right way. Both improve from using the six tips listed above!

The most important speeches we ever deliver are the ones delivered in a conflict with the most important audiences in our lives. Conflict management requires us to present our words with poise and confidence, and to present a helpful message adapted specifically to our audience.

Sometimes, we fail because we didn't properly prepare.

Have you ever said to someone close to you: "I am so sorry. I don't know what else to say other than I am sorry. I don't know why I acted like an idiot and said those shameful, angry, and regrettable words. I certainly didn't mean to, and I really don't believe what I said. I am sorry. I don't know why I was such an idiot to say exactly the wrong words at the wrong time."

I'll tell you why. You were thinking like an idiot! You see, when your image and identity are threatened (you hear, "You are NOT

O.K."), you automatically react with Fight or Flight. The hair on the back of your neck stands up, and your heart starts pumping blood, delivering oxygen to where you need it most for fighting or to take flight, your arms and legs.

Or, is that where you really need oxygen the most when engaged in interpersonal conflict? As your heart pumps to fill your arms and legs with blood, exactly where is it draining FROM? You bet. The one place you need an abundance of oxygen is in your brain. Instead, that oxygen is draining out of your head and into your feet. You search your brain for just the right words to manage this conflict. Your depleted brain makes a suggestion, and something stupid and idiotic comes spewing out of your mouth. Why? Because you are thinking like an idiot!

Anger Always Dissipates

Later you calm down. The adrenalin dissipates from your bloodstream. Soon, the blood and oxygen return to your brain. You begin thinking rationally instead of like some crazed primate in the jungle. Regretfully, the right words now come to mind and you begin, "I am so sorry…"

Prepare for a Challenge

Sometime, in the not too distant future, someone important to you is going to suggest you are not perfect in every way. They may insist you are NOT O.K. and need to change your behavior.

In the recent past, some of you may have had someone strongly suggest you were NOT O.K.! You may have heard those words, and immediately your heart started to pound, and you said, "Oh, you say I'm NOT O.K., well what about YOU!" And a battle of words has begun. Fighting words are hurled with the intensity and trajectory to inflict damage and pain. Aggressive verbal assaults, rapid-fire volleys of explosive and vindictive dialogue of shock and awe are delivered across clearly defined battle lines. Occasionally, it continues to escalate until some idiot unleashes a thermal nuclear bomb of vocabulary. Once those words are detonated on ground zero of an important person in your life, it is over. The poisonous fallout of your toxic words may have destroyed a once strong and powerful relationship.

The Most Common Abuse

I am mildly surprised why anyone would ever want to physically abuse a small child and leave scars that can last for years. Why physically abuse your kid when you can do a longer lasting job of destroying their self-image in ways that never leave a visible scar? Why not just verbally abuse your kids in both vivid and subtle ways that suggest they are NOT O.K. by your words instead of your actions? That verbal abuse will cripple them for years and possibly extend your abusive words to future generations. I have no doubt the most prevalent form of abuse is verbal.

One factor in how we choose to cope with conflict is how we were taught to manage our conflicts. Many of us have not had very good examples of how to manage conflict. And when words fail, that is when things get physical. If we can't find the right words, we can take things into our own hands. "I'll show you who is O.K. and who is NOT O.K.!"

I worry that some professionals in my audiences may be over-worked, under-paid, sleep-deprived, stressed-out, and in difficult personal relationships. These folks may have committed criminal violations of the law in their own homes in front of the most important people in their lives. Crimes committed because their words failed them, and they took matters into their own hands, briefly and violently.

But Not Everyone

Other professionals may have a complete opposite reaction to the words, "You are NOT O.K.!" They take flight. These folks instead say, "I do not have to listen to this; goodbye; talk to the back of my head as I stomp out that door and slam it in your face. Watch me as I jump into my vehicle and peel out of the driveway in a spray of gravel and cloud of dust. Watch me find some people who will tell me I am O.K.! And when I am done with those people telling me I am O.K., I am coming home. If I find you upstairs, Baby, I am going downstairs! If you come downstairs, then I am going upstairs. If I am in the same room with you, watch me stick my nose deep into my newspaper and become INVISIBLE. I am taking flight to someplace else because I don't have to listen to this ****!"

At this point, some faces in my audience are more somber and reflective than at any other point in the seminar. Some are looking at me with tilted heads and confused expressions suggesting they are wondering, "How do you know?"

I know the two options, Fight or Flight, are the two most natural, normal, and expected reactions to a threat by any mammal on the planet including *Homo Stupidus*. The reactions are mapped deep within our genetic heritage.

Some of us have a natural tendency toward one option and others of us toward the other. *The Villa Incident* illustrates the opposite tendencies to confront or avoid our conflicts.

Greek philosophers observed there is a third passive option by which you do neither: Surrender! Succumb to the inevitable and be eaten alive, conquered, or enslaved.

A Fourth Option

The ancient Greeks also had a special appreciation for the fourth option of managing the inevitable conflicts of civilized life. The middle ground between fighting and flight is the one thing that separates humans from all the other species in the jungle. The thing that makes us human is WORDS!

Some of us use our human intellect to find and say just the right words in the right way to manage our conflicts and create a just and proper outcome without violence and bloodshed.

The ancient Greeks taught us that great civilizations are founded and protected by citizens: "good men, speaking well." Extensive preparation and class time was devoted to teaching young citizens *rhetoric*—the persuasive use of words. The goal was to produce citizens capable of expertly using their words to manage their conflicts with diplomacy, eloquence, and without reaching for a sword.

THE CHAPTER CHALLENGE

My challenge to you is this. Sometime, in the not too distant future, someone who is important to you is going to suggest you are not perfect in every way. They may insist that you are NOT O.K.

Neither Fight nor Flight. Resist the temptation to passionately engage or passively avoid the conflict; neither attack nor retreat, and offer these words: "I will not fight with you, and I am not leaving this room."

Now that you have them either attentive or confused, say this: "Since I won't fight and I am not leaving, all that is left are my words. A wise professor once suggested that asking questions is our most important communication skill. So, let me ask you this question. How can I help resolve this conflict to your delight and satisfaction?"

Many of my participant's spouses who were confused moments ago are now certain this is not MY spouse. They may demand to know, "Just who are you? Why are you wearing my spouse's clothes, and what have you done with my spouse?"

Some partners expect their predictable Fighting Spouse or Taking Flight Spouse. In every conflict, their partner always does one or the other, and this new person does neither! They have never heard such words in a conflict, "How can I help?"

My participants may attempt such a strategy, but their partner may insist on engaging in their typical and predictable behaviors of either engagement or retreat. Lacking discipline, some may fall victim to the principle of reciprocity and talk to their partner exactly the way they are talking to them. "If they want to fight, I am game. They want to take flight and avoid discussions; fine, I can play that game too. In fact, I'll talk to them the same way they are talking to me."

The Next Challenge

Listen to yourself. Discipline your words, and instead say only the right words in the right way to manage the perception of differences with the most important people in your life.

Be a communication professional; model communication excellence, and demonstrate how a professional skillfully manages conflict.

Recall the six tips for managing speech anxiety? Those six tips are also appropriate for managing your conflicts:

1. Be prepared with a planned outline of thoughts.
2. Focus on what is most important
   (your audience, not your image).
3. Know your message.
4. Emphasize how your message will help.
5. Adapt to your particular audience.
6. Imagine how a confident and comfortable version of
   you would talk to this audience, and ACT like that!

Axioms of Conflict

An axiom is a universal truth—true for you and true for me. Here are three axioms related to conflict management:
1. You can't avoid conflict.
2. Perceived injustices are the root cause of conflict.
3. Most conflicts are with the people you care the most about!

The first axiom is obvious by the chapter definition of conflict—the expressed struggle between at least two parties who *perceive* incompatible goals, values, or beliefs. Conflict can also be a struggle with differing attitudes, scarce resources, or interference in achieving goals.

Competing goals, values, beliefs, and interference abound in life. No kidding. Conflict is inevitable, and you can't avoid conflict. Yet many of us continue to ignore the elephant in the living room. Unable to find the right words to manage their conflicts, some people would even pretend to act deaf to avoid confrontation. By avoiding a conflict that could have been easily managed on the east side of the road, they manage to almost get killed on the other side of the road because they kept avoiding the obvious conflict!

Perceived Injustices

Have you ever been in a conflict and then learned the one bit of information that changes your entire perception of the conflict? "Oh, I get it now. You really are on my side!" Then we repeat the words of Emily Litella, "Never mind!"

Perceived injustices are the cause of most conflicts. The problem was not that we had conflicting goals. We only had a perception that a wrong was done to us. Change of perceptions, instant resolution of the conflict.

Earlier, was there a true conflict between me and the pest control guy or merely the perception of competing goals?

You may also be, like many professional police officers, "unoffendable" no matter what someone might say. You may have never filed a formal complaint or demanded an apology from anyone for a word used in your presence. Have you ever wondered why some people regularly get offended? Have you ever wondered why there are so many letter writing, complaint filing, apology demanding, lawsuit filing, professional "victims" claiming perceived injustices? Why are some people eager to be offended?

Because it is rewarded! What is the reward for being offended by what someone says? The twin benefits of claiming offense are Victimization and Superiority. The offended get the attention accorded to the injured, AND they also get to look down their nose at the offender for such behavior. "Poor, poor me, AND I would never stoop so low..."

Some of us do not enjoy feeling "victimized," practice excessive tolerance of others, and avoid overt attempts to demonstrate moral superiority. By avoiding constant perceived injustices, those people manage to perceptually avoid many potential conflicts. They also live in happy homes, stay out of court, and stay away from complaining about every possible perceived personal injustice.

Most of Our Conflicts are with the Most Important People in Our Life

The nameless strangers in our audiences are not the people with whom we have most of our conflicts. The third and final axiom of conflict reminds us that most of our conflicts are with the most important people in our lives: the people we live and work with!

All of us could benefit from improving our conflict management skills. Understanding what your conflicts are *actually* about will help you in your efforts to manage conflict.

Two Concerns in Every Conflict

Every conflict with the important people in your life is about two conflicting concerns:

Concern for YOUR goals

Concern for THEIR goals

I am always surprised to hear conflict partners complain, "It's always all about you, your goals, your needs, your desires...what about me?" Of course it is about their goals competing with your goals or else you wouldn't have a conflict.

Many semesters, I required students to keep a journal of conflicts each experienced during the course of a month. Some would have a really thick journal at the end of the month! Then we would try to identify what the conflict was *really* about. The discussions revealed three conflicting goals were consistently identified regarding what the conflicts were *really* about:

CONTENT: I didn't GET what I wanted!

RELATIONSHIP: I wasn't TREATED how I wanted
    to be treated!

IDENTITY: I wasn't SEEN how I wanted to be seen!

No wonder conflicts seem to always be about THEIR goals. They are!

WHAT DO YOU WANT MORE THAN ANYTHING ELSE?

If you answered "a 19-foot metallic red Ranger bass fishing boat with a 200 horsepower outboard motor," then you are just like me! At least, just like me in January of 1993.

That January was my first as a university professor. I had taken the job after completing my Ph.D. the previous summer. Going back to college at age 31, with two young daughters, required an extreme financial sacrifice for three long years in Kansas for all four of us.

But this new year of 1993, with a steady paycheck, we were all beginning to reap rewards for our sacrifices. I had also begun doing off-campus seminars for my first clients. The occasional seminar check helped a lot given that the 1992 annual reward for an assistant professor in Arkansas was $28,500.

I turned down an offer for the position of professor at a San Antonio university partly because Arkansas is such a beautiful state and Little Rock is so close to mountains, streams, lakes, forests, and rivers. I envisioned that upon my arrival, I would soon take advantage of the numerous fishing opportunities in the state. I was delighted to learn a world-record brown trout was recently fished out of the nearby Little Red River, and the professional bass tours made numerous stops in lakes and rivers less than an hour from my front door. Mountain streams, just to the north, held trophy small-mouth bass. Monster catfish were available in the Mississippi and Arkansas Rivers, and 40-pound stripers were regularly caught in a number of my adopted state's deep reservoirs. Rainbow trout, by the thousands, were stocked in the cold tail waters below many of the local dams. The Natural State was a natural choice for a fisherman.

During my first January in Arkansas, I eagerly took my young family to the Arkansas Boat Show. Wide-eyed, we looked at the wide varieties of boats designed to float on every imaginable water in the state: huge houseboats, tiny kayaks, deck boats, flat bottom boats, ski boats, fishing boats, boats with bedrooms, boats you inflate, boats for bass, boats for stripers, boats for duck hunting, boats for rivers, boats for speed, and boats in every color of the most beautiful rainbow you have ever seen!

Then I saw the boat of my dreams displayed right before my eyes: a brand new 19-foot metallic red Ranger Bass boat mounted with a 200 horsepower motor! I pulled my family close and said, "That is why we sacrificed all those long, cold, hungry winters in the windy plains of Kansas. Girls, that boat is why we picked Arkansas." I looked at my smiling reflection in the polished fiberglass and metal that I knew would someday be mine. "Someday soon," I confidently whispered.

****

WHERE IS MY BOAT TODAY?

I'll tell you where my boat is today, still at the factory! In all these years, I have yet to take delivery. Why not? I can offer one possible explanation. I live with three women.

You may have had a similar experience as mine, raising two daughters. Great kids; wish I could afford more just like them but only if I had earned $28,500 each *month*.

Ranger Boats never delivered my boat because every month since 1993, some $100-$300 expense beyond food, shelter, and clothes for one of my two daughters would show up in my mailbox. A bill I wouldn't expect at the first of the month would be due the last of the month. Some months, it was bills for each: orthodontia, ballet lessons, soccer camps, or medical emergencies.

Each year, as I made more, the bills each month would get bigger: prom dresses, new cars, college tuition! So, I still don't have my boat.

That is one possible explanation for my unhappiness from not owning my Ranger Boat: my two daughters. It could be an attractive explanation for my unhappiness. I could blame my unhappiness on them. Could I potentially accept this version of events and claim a perceived injustice?

Of course I could. Then I would be free to constantly criticize and complain about my unhappiness, and every month I could remind my young daughters how expensive they are and how much they contribute to my unhappiness over not getting to buy the fishing boat of my dreams.

Sure, I *could* buy into that perceived injustice and even produce a mountain of evidence to defend and support my claims. I could belittle and blame the most important people in my life for my unhappiness. It could be an attractive option.

Who is Really to Blame for My Unhappiness?

I could blame my daughters, but every participant in my seminars knows who is really to blame. The one person I should be blaming is the one person most responsible for my unhappiness. You know who that person is: my wife!

My wife must be the one to blame for my unhappiness. I saw both of my daughters come right out of her. If there is anyone to blame, it must be *her* fault if I am unhappy. Right?

Relationship Goals

Earlier, I asked: What do you want? If you answered with "a loving, trusting, caring relationship that would last a lifetime," well then, you are just like me. You may also be in a 30-plus year relationship. And, like me, you may also know that blaming others for your unhappiness is a terrific way to end a relationship in 30 seconds.

My wife, Melissa, the one true love of my life, has some relationship goals and beliefs. For example, she believes husbands must always tell the truth and keep their wives informed about where they are, what they are doing, and who they are doing it with 24 hours a day! Can you imagine such difficult relationship goals to satisfy for 30 years? Of course, it might be tempting to just lead her to believe she knows exactly where I am, who I am with, and what I am doing. Tell her exactly what she wants to hear and only what I want her to know, conveniently forgetting to include a specific detail or two.

In this relationship I have enjoyed with my wife, I have also learned the best way to deal with people is to give them what they want. Not the *perception*, but give them exactly what they want. That, I have found, has made it A LOT easier for me to maintain an important relationship for decades. As it turns out, I have learned I am just like her! Melissa and I both have the same goal of being kept informed about the most important people in our life.

As I would review my student's conflict journals, it appeared that most of their conflicts were not about not getting what they want but rather violations of their personal relationship goals. The ongoing conflicts focused much more on not getting treated the way they preferred in an important relationship. Judging from some of these relationships in the conflict journals I'd review, it appeared some will never learn, even in 30 years of hard lessons, the easiest way to get what you want is to give others exactly what they want.

IDENTITY GOALS

A surprising number of my young students' conflicts were about neither content nor relationship goals. Many of the conflicts began with someone suggesting, "You are NOT O.K.!" and a defensive posture was instinctively taken. Words don't even have to be heard, "I just did not like the way he was looking at me," was often written in the journals. "So then, I said…" So begins the familiar spiral of engagement and retreat because someone suggested someone else wasn't perfect in every way: not punctual enough, sympathetic enough, forthcoming enough; too demanding, insecure, or inattentive.

Students would occasionally write heartbreaking tales of slights, confrontation, and decimation of their self-image and public image in the eyes of some of the most important people in their lives. Daily, and for weeks, the student journals included refrains suggesting, "You are not important, you are stupid, or you are not appreciated," coming from a parent. Then, a few pages later, they would write about a conflict with their boyfriend or girlfriend, and I would see the same angry accusations and condemnations, once again, only this time the hostile words were said by the journal-writing student.

The best advice my students taught me for managing relationship goals and AVOIDING conflicts with the most important people in your life is to give difficult people what they want and remember these principles:

Everyone wants to be important,
No one wants to look stupid,
Everyone wants to be appreciated,
And never criticize, condemn, or complain about the most important people in your life.

Four Possible Conflict Outcomes

Every conflict, big or small, interpersonal or international, ends in one of four outcomes for the parties involved:

You Win - They Lose
You Lose - They Win
You Lose - They Lose
You Win - They Win

The only way we can lead a successful WIN-WIN outcome is if the other party sees themselves as winning. So, your primary conflict strategy is to help your partner see that you are giving them EXACTLY what they want, to see themselves as winning in the conflict over perceived incompatibility of goals.

You Win – They Lose

This is a competitive style of conflict. Sports are designed to create exactly this W/L outcome. Both competitors want to win, but both can't. So, somebody has to lose.

Or, do they? Some competitors' philosophy is, "It isn't whether we win or lose, it is all in how we play the game. If we did our best, we are satisfied to have competed!"

Some would suggest the philosophy above is that of a loser. "Winning is everything and winning is the only thing," the conquerors proclaim from the victory stand.

In some relationships, the strategy is to simply make my partner feel like a loser, and I Win! The competitor freely uses personal criticism, rejects others' feelings and beliefs, blames others, refuses responsibility, and makes hostile threats and demands. The goal is to WIN at all costs. Tony Soprano has perfected the art of competition when he makes you an offer "you can't refuse"!

The problem with Win-Lose is obvious: it creates losers. That may be acceptable in sports but is not O.K. in most personal and professional relationships. Threats, verbal hostility, criticisms, condemnation, complaints, and physical violence are great tools to help the committed competitor to WIN the battle at all costs.

If your partner also chooses to use this competitive style, in the words of Tony Soprano, "This injustice must be repaid."

You Lose – They Win

The flip side of winning is losing, and that sucks. No one wants to feel like a loser.

But the strategy of Accommodation is the most *efficient* conflict ending style available. If your primary goal is to simply END the conflict, then this is your style. It only requires that you cave in to the often excessive and repeated demands of others, and just give them everything they want.

The beauty of accommodation is that it works. If I stick a gun in your back, you will give me exactly what I want! Fortunately, although they hold our lives in the balance, most of the important people in our lives are only asking to feel important, look smart, and get some appreciation. In those cases, you can afford to accommodate, many others you cannot.

Losing your wallet sucks, and so does losing control over your life. I am proud my family can be described as accommodating. We are all very agreeable, easy to get along with, and have difficulty refusing requests for our cooperation. It may be partially genetic.

Delaware Tribe of Indians

My daughters and I are voting members of the Delaware Tribe of Indians based in Bartlesville, Oklahoma. Geography students may find it ironic to learn the Delaware Tribe is based in Oklahoma. Shouldn't they be based in Delaware or near the Delaware River between New Jersey and Pennsylvania in the Mid-Atlantic region of the east coast? Why Oklahoma? Oklahoma is now home to the Delawares because in the 1600's, the Delawares were a very accommodating tribe of Native Americans. This accommodating tribe welcomed the Quakers, the Dutch, and the English to their lands on the Mid-Atlantic coast. William Penn was dependent on the natives as he began his Great Experiment and founded the city of Brotherly Love on the ancestral lands of these Native Americans. Things got crowded; brotherly love dissipated; the Delawares accommodated and moved a little west. Then the tribe moved a little further and accommodated themselves all the way across the Appalachian Mountains into Ohio. Then many of the tribe moved on further to Indiana, Missouri, eventually Kansas, and finally to Oklahoma in the 1860's.

The classic accommodation consequence: Give an inch and they will take a mile. The Delawares accommodated themselves out of house and homeland.

You Lose – They Lose

This is the avoidant style of conflict management. You tiptoe around the elephant in the living room never mentioning that the pachyderm is a problem for you. You change the topic, deny a problem exists, or postpone discussions until later. The problem isn't confronted, and it's possible that by avoiding the problem you set the stage for an explosive response later.

Of course, sometimes the problem is no big deal, or it is a big deal and you need some time to plan your response, or the costs associated with engagement may be too high. Other times, both parties agree implicitly or openly to avoid those topics. On those occasions, the most appropriate style may be avoidance.

Other times, in intimate relationships, one party practices *nonconsensual avoidance* with another party. "I am not going to talk about it," proclaims a withdrawing and avoidant husband to his frustrated and confused wife. This type of behavior is dissatisfying to the spouse and often destructive to the relationship. Supervisors, parents, and intimate partners occasionally get stuck in the avoidant pattern. Afraid to say the wrong thing, they eventually say nothing. Dissatisfied employees seek employment elsewhere; greater distance grows between parent and child; month-to-month intimacy disappears in once intimate relationships. Everyone loses when we are either unwilling or unable to constructively manage our conflicts.

EVERYBODY LOSES

In 1791, President George Washington was devastated to learn of what is still the largest loss of American military lives in a battle with Native Americans. In western Ohio, an alliance of displaced Native American tribes attacked an American army unit killing 600 men and wounding 400. In the nation's then capitol of Philadelphia, President George Washington exploded in a rage when told the peaceful and accommodating Delaware tribe of Indians were part of the Ohio massacre.

The term massacre is rarely applied to the killing of Native Americans, but it is appropriately applied to the prior Gnadenhuetten Massacre of 90 Delaware Indians in 1781. In the western Ohio town of Gnadenhutten, 100 converted Christian Delaware Indians had peacefully settled far west of their former problems with the whites on the east coast. Motivated by protection, a small group of Delawares settled in Gnadenhuetten and adopted the customs and religion of the local missionaries. In March of 1781, a Pennsylvania militia group from Washington County arrested and escorted 90 Delawares from their homes and cornfields. With the Delawares locked in their church, a vote was taken whether to take the prisoners back to their fort or kill them. The decision was overwhelmingly in favor of execution. The Christian Delawares spent the night praying and singing hymns. In the morning, two slaughter houses were selected, and the Christian Delawares—29 men, 27 women, and 34 children—were taken inside by soldiers in small groups, forced to kneel, and then had their skulls crushed with heavy wooden mallets. Afterwards, the troops burned the town. They then loaded up all the plunder available from their victims and took it home with them to their wives and children in Pennsylvania.

Years later, the Delawares were forced out of Kansas and into Indian Territory. The new "Free State" was admitted to the Union (part of the Missouri Compromise favored by Abraham Lincoln as a move to avoid a civil war with the slave holding states). The invading settlers required more accommodation of the tribe, and the federal government sent the tribe packing to Oklahoma.

****

Everyone loses when we avoid managing our conflicts because we are either unwilling or unable to constructively manage conflict.

You Win – They Win

The most constructive style of conflict management is collaboration. This style demonstrates high concern for both your goals and the goals of others. The conflict doesn't conclude unless both parties are satisfied they are getting what they want. So, you cannot create a WIN-WIN outcome until the other *perceives* he is winning. This style demands discipline and your best communication skills. Discipline, because most us of are inclined to go along with our partners style, "If she wants to fight, then a fight it will be," or "If he wants to withdraw into his own little world, fine, I'll let him sit. I will not talk to him the same way he is not talking to me."

Heightened verbal skills are required because if you are not going to fight and if you are not going to avoid the subject, the only constructive option you have is your words. You are going to have to self disclose; you are going to make descriptive statements of wants; you are going to ask for cooperation. Above all else, you are going to get what you want because you are going to give them what they want. You will demonstrate respect for the other person and their goals, values, and beliefs.

With a collaborative style, you will accept responsibility for the ultimate successful resolution of the conflict. You will model communication excellence in all of your stressful interactions; you will ask good questions; you will do all you can to help your partner perceive himself or herself as a winner before you make any requests for what it is you want.

CHAPTER SEVEN REVIEW:
CONFLICT MANAGEMENT

Conflict was defined as:
the expressed struggle between parties who perceive incompatible goals, values, and beliefs.

Conflict management is perception management.

Emergencies are situations with outcomes you perceive as important and unknown.

The physiological response to an emergency is called *Fight or Flight.*

Six Quick Tips to Cope With Speech Anxiety:
- *Be prepared with a planned outline of thoughts.*
- *Focus on what is most important (your audience, not your image).*
- *Know your message.*
- *Emphasize how your message will help.*
- *Adapt to your particular audience.*
- *Imagine how a confident and comfortable version of you would talk to this audience, and ACT like that!*

The Fight or Flight Reaction drains oxygen from your brain leading you to say something only an idiot would say.

Axioms of Conflict Management:
- *You can't avoid conflict.*
- *Perceived injustices are the root cause of conflict.*
- *Most conflicts are with the people you care the most about!*

Common Conflicting Goals:
Content: *I didn't get what I wanted.*
Relationship: *I wasn't treated how I wanted to be treated.*
Identity: *I wasn't seen how I wanted to be seen.*

Four Conflict Outcomes:
You Win - They Lose   You Lose - They Win
You Lose - They Lose   You Win - They Win

Best advice for avoiding conflict: *Give them what they want!*

EIGHT
Ancient Principles
of Persuasion

Think back a long time ago. Now think even further back in time, a long, long time ago.

Are you thinking about the year 350 B.C.? If not, start thinking about it now because we are going to be spending some time in the year 350 B.C.

In this chapter, I will introduce you to some principles about getting others to do what you want them to do that were suggested by ancient philosophers thousands of years ago. The two thousand year-old advice is from Aristotle's *Rhetorica* written in 350 B.C. (as best we can estimate).

I sometimes worry if ancient Greek philosophy is appropriate content for my audiences. I often ask, by a show of hands, how many in my audience have recently read Aristotle's great contribution to Western literature?

Since few ever raise their hand, I share a brief summary of the principles of persuasion found in ancient Greek philosophy.

I HAVE A PROBLEM WITH DALE CARNEGIE

Actually, he is O.K.! I only have a problem with the words on the cover of my copy of Dale Carnegie's *How To Win Friends and Influence People*. It seems that, on my cover, right between the title and author's name, there are words claiming this book is the first book of its kind to lead you to success. Unfortunately, Dale Carnegie missed that claim by over 20 centuries. Aristotle's *Rhetorica* is something of a guide for the masses in their efforts to say the right thing at the right time, to be a model citizen, to speak as a sophisticated citizen, and to win friends and influence people without resorting to physical violence.

Do you recall the book an officer in Lubbock loaned me? It was a copy of Dale Carnegie's 1932 book on Abraham Lincoln. Remember, the book was the apparent basis and outline for the later 1935 publication *How To Win Friends and Influence People*. Now then, if Lincoln was the model for all of the principles for Dale Carnegie's book on influence and success, when and where did Lincoln get those principles? Certainly not from his illiterate father whose funeral Lincoln neglected to attend, nor his mother who died early in his childhood.

Lincoln found the principles in the words written in the classic literature available to a child of the wilderness: Socrates, Plato, and Aristotle. The principles and words Lincoln used to change the world were found in the writings of the ancient Greek philosophers: The ideal of everyone having a voice in the government—*Demos Kratia*, the people rule; argumentation and debate rise to an art form; representatives are elected and Senates are formed; laws are enacted by the people rather than by edict from a dictator.

Think about the year 350 B.C. and imagine that I am an average Athenian who is angry with my neighbor because he is doing something that bothers me. Now, in the year 350 B.C., you might expect my angry response would be to march over and chop his head off—end of problem.

In a nearby academy, Aristotle is teaching his students the principles of Rhetoric: the persuasive use of words to encourage cooperation verbally. I think it is a shame that a fine word like *rhetoric* has, over the centuries, gathered pejorative usage in the description of political and other discussions as a bunch of "rhetoric!"

I assume the ancient Greek philosophers would also be dismayed to learn of rhetoric being used dismissively. Take a look at these words:

John 1:1 - In the beginning was the Word, and the Word was with God, and the Word was God.

If I could ask Aristotle to tell me what those words mean to him, I trust he would interpret the biblical writings to support his worldview. He would argue that the human experience begins with the word, and that the defining characteristic of human beings is that we alone can use words to manage our interactions with one another. No other specie can use words. If words are what make us human, then that which makes us human is sacred. Aristotle believed if we are to be a better human, we must become better at using the one thing that makes us human: our words.

Let's say way back in 350 B.C., I am enrolled in Aristotle's academy, and one day, the lecture is on rhetoric. I interrupt the great philosopher's lecture and ask, "Sure use your words, but just exactly how can I use my words to get my annoying neighbor to stop doing what he does that bothers me so? I am tempted to pull out my sword and chop his head off. Please sir, tell me what words I can say to get him to stop doing what he is doing?"

I am absolutely certain Aristotle would have responded with a question, "Have you asked your neighbor for his cooperation?" I am so certain he would ask because his former teacher, Plato, would have instilled the principle he learned from his mentor, Socrates: Your most important verbal skill is the question! The principle is known in academia as the Socratic Method of Inquiry. How do you get cooperation from others? ASK.

Aristotle would remind me that if I ask for my neighbor's cooperation, he has three likely ways to respond. First, he may agree to cooperate. Second, he may refuse to cooperate, but the final option is his most likely choice. He asks, "Why, why should I cooperate? What is in it for me?"

THE RHETORICAL MOMENT

Now you are in the Rhetorical Moment. Because, Aristotle would argue, if you can overcome his implied objection, you can win his cooperation. Your goal is to help your neighbor perceive that his cooperation will be rewarded. The challenge is to convince your neighbor his cooperation will be in *his* best interest.

"Why should I cooperate?" your neighbor asks. Aristotle taught that when you answer the question, your answer should reflect *Logos, Pathos,* and *Ethos.* Now if that looks Greek to you, it should. Let's look at each in detail.

RATIONAL EXPLANATION

When Aristotle spoke of *Logos,* he was referring to Logic. Answer the question with a logical, rational explanation as to why your neighbor should cooperate. The original Greek academies spent a great deal of class time examining syllogisms, enthymemes, and logical fallacies so a citizen could present cogent and rational arguments as to why their neighbors should cooperate with a citizen's requests.

WHEN LOGIC FAILS

When logic fails, don't reach for your sword. Instead, try making an appeal to *Pathos.* While *Logos* is found in the head, *Pathos* resides in the heart. Emotional appeals are designed to make your neighbor *feel* the need to cooperate. Even if you convince them logically that your proposition is a good idea, audiences typically aren't going to be moved to action unless they feel motivated. *Logos* and *Pathos* work to compliment one another: my proposition is the smart thing to do, AND it will feel good to cooperate! You involve your audience psychologically and physiologically with logical arguments and emotional appeals.

Lots of emotional appeals are available: patriotism, altruism, security, self-esteem, and health. Emotions speakers may arouse are anger, envy, jealousy, love, or pride. Advertisers play on these emotions in attempts to get you to cooperate and buy their products—you do not want yellow teeth; you do not want spots on your dishes; you do not want to lose your hair. But you do want to look smart, be envied, and have long, silky, beautiful, manageable hair, don't you?

Aristotle recognized the most powerfully motivating emotion is fear. People are in constant fear of two things: the fear of not getting what they want (Pleasure) and the fear of getting something they do not want (Pain).

Imagine I was king of a powerful country, and I didn't like what some other dictator was doing in his country. I insisted he stop doing the things that bother me. My closest advisors warn me of the dictator's dangerous weapons and evil intentions. Let's say the evil dictator hesitates, procrastinates, and ultimately refuses to cooperate. I decide I need to "chop his head off." In a democracy, I would need my citizens' permission. I may be tempted to use seemingly justifiable fear tactics to encourage their cooperation in my goals. I could convince them the uncooperative dictator is someone they should FEAR! I could fearfully warn of weapons the foreign dictator has available to likely unleash mass destruction on the very citizens I am asking to support me in my goals.

Then if my logical arguments fail but my fear tactics are successful in securing permission from those citizens, I had better hope I can produce evidence my fear tactics were justified. Because citizens today, just as thousands of years ago, resent when their voice in government has been quieted by fear tactics and unjustified emotional appeals. Leaders throughout history have suffered blows to their credibility and public image when questions arise about the true motive for their actions.

When All Else Fails, Try Ethos

Now, I imagine if I were a leader looking for a justification to start a competitive conflict, I would begin and end every argument as Abraham Lincoln did. "Why cooperate with me? Because it is the RIGHT THING TO DO." I would make an appeal to do the ethical thing, the right thing, and stand up to the wrong. "So, citizens, it may not seem like the smart thing to do; it may not feel like the right thing to do; but to do nothing when we could would be wrong." I would argue, "What I am asking you to do is the right thing to do."

Lincoln was commander-in-chief of an army dedicated to destroying fellow Americans. Tens of thousands of causalities mounted on both sides. Soldiers were being killed in battles for weeks and months on end. Over 600,000 Americans died in the Civil War. The President was vilified to let such mass destruction continue, but he felt he must continue the war. The justification that guided Lincoln through his darkest days was that to do nothing to save the Union was wrong, and the war was the right thing to do. Lincoln saw the young United States, only four score and seven years old, as a beacon of the hope of freedom and democracy for future generations worldwide and believed it was his duty to do all in his power to preserve the Union.

Most discussions of *Ethos* focus on the social construct of credibility: the speaker's public image and identity. Speaker credibility is often synonymous with the Aristotelian ideal of Ethos: "a good man, speaking well." The speaker has high credibility with his audience because he is seen as knowledgeable, experienced, familiar, and trustworthy. However, the most critical component of character that bestows credibility on a speaker is goodwill. The speaker has repeatedly demonstrated he is a "good man" with no selfish motives and has only his audience's best interest at heart; the speaker is asking for cooperation because he is only trying to help.

Why are so many willing to do what Jesus wants us to do? Because they are convinced he is only motivated by his followers' best interest and would never ask them to do anything that wasn't.

A request for cooperation that is supported by logical argument, feels good to do, and is coming from a credible speaker who has my best interest at heart is an easy request to honor. Many of us are inclined to cooperate with those speakers who have us convinced our cooperation is the right thing to do.

How Do You Get Cooperation?

The ancient Greek philosophers suggested you first ask. Then you explain. You can start with an ethical appeal: It is the right thing to do, and here are my arguments why. If that fails, try a rational appeal: It makes logical sense; it is the smart thing to do!

"Hell no, I ain't cooperating," says your reluctant neighbor.

If your request fails, chop his head off. You asked nicely. Twice! Why not chop his head off? Because Aristotle and Socrates both noted that successful people ask, ask, and keeping asking until they are successful.

Next you could try a practical appeal, "It will work out better for the rest of us—your friends, neighbors, and loved ones—if you cooperate. Things will work better on a practical level. It is in everyone's best interest for you to cooperate."

The *Rhetorica* lists another dozen Aristotelian Rhetorical Appeals available to the rhetorician in attempts to generate voluntary compliance and influence people. But in those pages of ancient writings is the single most powerful Aristotelian Rhetorical Appeal available to get others to do what we want. Instead of reviewing all of the possible appeals, let me introduce the one most powerful appeal.

But First a Story

It is funny how just one phone call can change your entire life. More often, one call can screw up your whole week. Let me share a story about such a phone call.

THE SIXTEENTH STUDENT

One Monday morning, years ago, I was sitting in my campus office doing what professors do before the semester starts. This Monday was just 48 hours before the start of the new school year. Then my phone rang, and my week was about to get interesting.

The call was from Admissions and Records requesting my permission to add a 16th student to one of my courses that semester: Business and Professional Speaking. The B&P course was an advanced public speaking course. The curriculum was designed to give students as much experience presenting to audiences of fellow students that a 15-week semester would allow. The University set an enrollment limit of 15 students because B&P was a performance class. The fewer students in the class, the more experience each student receives in the semester.

Upon receiving the request for a 16th student, I immediately denied it. I explained to the admissions office that it is in everyone's best interest to decline all requests to exceed the 15-student enrollment.

Two minutes later, my phone rang. I answered a second call from the admissions office; this time the voice belonged to the Director of Admissions and Records. After identifying himself, he wanted to know if I knew exactly which student I was preventing from stepping into my classroom. I had to admit that I did not, but now I was curious. He said, "An administrative assistant in your college, Diane Soenso!"

I knew this particular administrator from a couple of task forces and college committees that we had both served on in prior years. She enthusiastically came prepared with the right answers to any problem our students or campus might face. Diane was also never the quietest, happiest, or the most popular person in any room she was in.

Faced with the prospect that my semester would include my boss's, boss's, boss's assistant, I stood my ground and said, "Sorry, the administrator is being treated the same as any student on campus."

The admissions director huffed, "Well, O.K.!" and abruptly hung up.

I stood and marched down the hall to my boss's office and began, "I just got off the phone with admissions…" After my description of the class enrollment issue, my Department Chair assured me that I had nothing to worry about. As professor, I did not have to change my rules for anyone.

He concluded, "Don't give it a second thought."

So, I didn't. When I stepped into my Business and Professional Speaking classroom the next Thursday afternoon, how many students did I find sitting in Room 201?

If you guessed SIXTEEN, then I guess you know someone like Diane Soenso, someone who just can't take NO for an answer.

I turned to my 15 students and said, "I forgot something in my office. I'll be right back!"

I sprinted down the hall to my boss's office and huffed, "You said not to give it a second thought, and now I have 16 students in room 201!"

He threw down what he had in his hand and pounded his desk, "Of course! Diane! I should have anticipated this." He told me to relax and that he was going to personally take care of my problem. He would talk to the Dean, resolve the problem, and I should concentrate on teaching the 15 students on my roster. I thanked him and rushed back to class.

That Thursday night, as I lay in bed next to the most wonderful woman in my life, the one true love of my life, my wife Melissa, who was the one woman I was laying there thinking about? Diane!

The next morning, I got up and went to campus with Diane on my mind. I taught my Friday classes, kept my office hours, and went to lunch with colleagues. Finally, late Friday afternoon, I caught my department chair in his office and I asked, "So?"

He looked up to see me standing in his office doorway with an inquisitive look on my face. He said, "Brian, of course. I just came back from a long discussion with the Dean about the B&P class and you and Diane. We talked about it and…" He paused to pat a chair in his office and continued, "Why don't you have a seat here, and I will tell you all about our discussion."

I had a dreadful feeling come over me as I took a seat and looked into the face of a man with a chagrinned expression. I immediately knew I was teaching 16 students that semester. My boss explained, "I am not sure who did Diane's last performance review, but whoever did strongly recommended she get some public speaking training. Off the record, the Dean and I agree with that recommendation. She could benefit from the class. The Dean and I also recognize Diane is going to be a special student, no doubt about that. We also know that it is going to take a very special and talented professor to help her with her problem. So…"

I didn't need to hear any more. I rose from my seat, expressed appreciation for all the "help" and began the long walk back to my office. Heavy with the burden of the prospect of teaching 16 students, I made it halfway down the hall when I remembered that I am something of an expert in dealing with difficult people, and I actually teach conflict management and negotiation. Plus, I am a competitor and I enjoy a challenge. Diane, I decided, would be my next persuasive challenge.

I marched into my office, picked up the phone, and dialed Diane's office. Before I could take a breath, Diane answered and I said, "Diane, this is Brian Polansky. Can we have a brief visit this afternoon?"

She said, "Oh my, can it wait until Monday? I have a meeting downstairs in 15 minutes."

"It won't take me but a minute to get there, and I promise I won't take up more than two minutes of your time," I assured her.

Diane relented, "Well, you better leave now and hurry."

I hung up the phone and sprinted out of my office. I picked up speed as I crossed campus and neared the administration building. At the top of the stairs leading to the administration building, I grabbed hold of the doorknob and stopped to ask myself an obvious question, "What is your communication plan here, Professor? What are you going to say to get Diane to do what you want?" Standing out in the hot August Friday afternoon sunshine, I did a quick review of the Aristotelian Appeals.

I considered an ethical appeal whereby I would explain there is the right thing to do and the wrong thing to do. I could argue that what Diane is doing in my classroom is wrong, wrong, wrong. I rejected that plan and considered another.

I could use a logical appeal and tell her there are smart things to do and there are stupid things to do, and what she is doing is stupid. I rejected that plan even quicker, and I considered another.

I could use a practical appeal and explain that it would work out better for the professor and his 15 students if they do not have a campus administrator in the class, and that it would work better for the rest of us in the room if she would quit showing up. Another rejection. By now, I was beginning to sweat a persuasive answer as to why she should cooperate with my request for her to stop attending my class.

Finally, doorknob in hand and with perspiration dripping down my forehead, I recalled the single most powerful Aristotelian Rhetorical Appeal. Armed with this appeal, I knew exactly what I was going to say.

I confidently swung open that door and marched down the corridor into Diane's office. I stepped into an impressive office of leather and oak in traditional academic décor with diplomas and certificates prominently displayed. She stepped from behind her desk and said, "So, I assume you came over to talk to me about your class."

"Oh my no," I exclaimed. "I rushed over here because I want to tell you how very impressed I am with you and your interest in attending my B&P class. I am impressed with any administrator who is willing to leave the ivory towers of academia and sit shoulder to shoulder, once again, with students in a classroom. I am particularly impressed with your interest in the study of public speaking. It is a lifelong study, and I applaud anyone who is willing to commit to a semester of study and criticism. I am also very impressed with your specific choice of professor. I am flattered and delighted to help you with your problem.

"However, since your time is short, let me make one simple little request and I'll be gone. My request is this: Will you please quit showing up in my classroom?" Now, if you know a Diane, then you know the look on this Diane's face right about then.

I explained, "I ask because you are not going to get what you think you are going to get out of that class. You see, that class is specifically designed to give 15 young college students as much experience in public speaking as possible in 15 weeks. From what I understand, you are an experienced public speaker. Your job gives you plenty of experience presenting to audiences. I am sure you don't need a class for the experience, but I am guessing you could benefit from some coaching. As your coach, I would come to one of your regularly scheduled campus presentations and sit in the back with an evaluation sheet. I would listen and make notes about your strengths, identify some things for you to avoid, and make some suggestions about how you might improve your presentations."

I continued, "I have helped several others in the past, just like you, who have the opportunity to professionally develop with their own audiences, their own message, and their own personal coach. Allow me to serve you as your coach, and I'll make you a better public speaker in two or three sessions rather than 15 weeks. Diane, can we reach an understanding? You will quit showing up in my classroom, and the next time you have a campus presentation you will pick up that phone and invite me to serve as your coach."

She exclaimed, "Now, that is exactly what I am looking for!"

I said, "Then I will eagerly await your call," and then quickly exited into the bright Friday afternoon.

****

What is the single most powerful Aristotelian Appeal available?

THE PERSONAL APPEAL

People don't comply because YOU want them to.
People don't comply because YOU think it is a good idea.
And they don't comply because YOU really feel like they should or even because it would be in YOUR best interest. People comply because they believe THEIR cooperation is in THEIR best interest!

Therefore, you must craft your logical, emotional, and practical appeals to satisfy your audience's personal needs, wants, and goals. The greater the personal satisfaction that compliance provides your audience, the greater the likelihood you will get compliance from your audience.

How do you get someone to confess to capital murder? Convince them a confession is in their best interest!

If I know exactly what it is you want and can demonstrate that your cooperation will get you what you want, then history has repeatedly demonstrated that I can get you to do remarkable, miraculous, and heroic deeds. History has also shown that those who can give people what they want can also generate compliance to commit incredibly horrible and violent acts.

Why people do what they do is the focus of the next chapter.

CHAPTER EIGHT REVIEW:
ANCIENT PRINCIPLES OF PERSUASION

Aristotle believed if we are to be a better human,
  we must become better at using the one thing that
  makes us human: *our words.*

The Socratic Method demonstrates the importance of
  asking questions as an important verbal skill.

The Rhetorical Moment is the moment your audience asks,
  "Why should I cooperate, and what is in it for me?"

Emotions speakers may arouse include anger, love, pride,
  patriotism, altruism, and security.

The most powerfully motivating emotion is fear.

People fear two things:
  the fear of not getting what they want (pleasure)
  the fear of getting something they do not want (pain)

The three modes of persuasion suggested by Aristotle were:
  ❑ Logos – *the use of logical appeals*
  ❑ Pathos – *the use of emotional appeals*
  ❑ Ethos – *the use of speaker credibility*

Rhetoricians are encouraged to use:
  ❑ Ethical Appeals – *It would be the RIGHT thing to do*
  ❑ Rational Appeals – *It would be the SMART thing to do*
  ❑ Emotional Appeals – *It would FEEL good to do*
  ❑ Practical Appeals – *It would be better for OTHERS*
  ❑ Personal Appeals – *It would be in YOUR best interest*

Speakers with high credibility are perceived as familiar,
  knowledgeable, competent, and motivated by good will.

NINE
WHY DO PEOPLE DO WHAT THEY DO?

Now, that is a good question!

Long before 350 B.C., social scientists have tried to answer this question. Because if I know WHY you do what you do, then I know HOW to get you to do what I want you to do!

Social scientists, since the beginning of time, have sought valid and reliable explanations (theories) to explain human behavior. Let me introduce you to the three theories I have found to best explain human behavior. A basic understanding of these three theories will help you in your efforts to say the right words at the right time to encourage voluntary compliance.

UNCERTAINTY REDUCTION THEORY

This theory suggests that curiosity is the answer to the question of why people do what they do. We are all curious, questioning, inquisitive little creatures. What best explains human behavior? The insatiable need for certainty, a craving for knowledge, and an inherent dissatisfaction with the unknown explains a lot of human behavior.

Uncertainty Reduction Theory explains why we need theories. We need certainty about how, what, when, where, and why things are the way they are in our world. Certainty is attractive. Certainty is comforting. Certainty also provides prediction, and with prediction comes control, and with control we get what we want!

This theory suggests that our need to reduce uncertainty keeps us awake at night asking, "Why me...why this...why now?" Uncertainty reduction further suggests that the questions of "How can I...How should I...and How am I...?" function to get us out of bed and marching out the front door in the morning to find the answers to our uncertain lives.

This theory also explains why sixteen year-olds don't ask questions. There is a lot of satisfaction in presuming you have all the answers. The comfort provided by absolute certainty is tempting when considered against the confusion of uncertainty. The most common lies are the lies we tell ourselves in an effort to reduce uncertainty. We often selectively ignore an unattractive certainty like admitting, "I was wrong." Instead, we seek certainty by lying to ourselves about our shortcomings and fall victim to the Fundamental Perceptual Error: I see things as they are.

While this theory is based largely in Logos in that we seek rational explanations to satisfy cognitive needs, the Pathos that certainty provides cannot be denied. It feels good when we are certain we have all the answers.

Did I Mention That You are Going to Die?

I am certain of that. We don't like to think about that because of the cognitive dissonance associated with the certainty of our death. We cope by avoiding the topic because death is a downer. You probably haven't considered that right now you are closer to death than you have ever been in your entire life. What is the MOST uncertain question we ask ourselves about our death?

When? Nope.
Where? Nope
How? Nope.
Why? Nope.

Somewhere today, someone near you committed an act of suicide or murder. They had all of the answers to the questions above for either themselves or their victim: When, Where, How, and Why. But both victims, when faced with the certainty of death, probably still had one uncertain question left unanswered.

WHAT HAPPENS NEXT?

Since the beginning of time, people have been trying to provide audiences a satisfying explanation to this almost unanswerable question. Actually dying and going to the other side is the only certain way to answer the question of what happens next. Since most us are neither certain or curious enough to take matters into our own hands, we are left with some uncertainty and a lot of faith.

Our faith informs us of what awaits, but you have to faithfully accept the explanation without absolute certainty. You accept on faith. Throughout history and across cultures, we have been presented with alternative answers to the uncertain question of what happens next.

Some folks are absolutely certain they have got it right. They have all the answers, and they gather uncertain and curious audiences and give them what they want: certainty!

WHY DID THEY DO THAT?

On that bright, sunny afternoon of September 11, 2001 most of us were searching for a satisfying answer to the question above. Why would terrorists hijack four planes and crash into buildings with the certainty they were going to kill themselves and thousands of others? Why? I believe uncertainty reduction helps explain.

In the following days, we learned about Al Qaida and their terrorist organization that recruits impressionable young men and convinces them that if they do this horrible and unjust act of murder/suicide, here is what Allah has waiting for them in paradise: 72 dark-haired virgins!

How do you recruit suicide hijackers? Again, you give them what they want: certainty that cooperation is in their best interest.

Why does everyone love talking to my friend, Ralph? Because Ralph gives everyone what they want: the certainty that someone thinks they are O.K.!

Why do I do all I can to convince both my daughters that I think they are perfect in every way? Because if young girls doubt that the most important man in their life thinks they are O.K., then they will find another man to give them the answer they want.

Uncertainty Reduction Theory is the first of three explanations of human behavior. Now, let's look at another.

MASLOW'S HIERARCHY OF NEEDS

Most of my participants have been introduced to this theory long before they step into my seminar. This is one of the most popular theories available to explain why we do what we do—It feels good. This theory is based almost wholly on Pathos: We feel a need to do what we do. Some behaviors have no basis in logic, but they sure are pleasurable. Many of our biggest mistakes were the times we succumbed to emotional response rather than rational thought.

Abraham Maslow's theory suggests there is a hierarchy of human needs, and the lower needs have to be met before the higher needs serve as a motivator. He further suggests that once a need has been met, it no longer serves as a motivator.

PHYSICAL NEEDS

The hierarchy begins with a base of physiological needs that have to be met first. Those needs include water, food, and air. In every audience, I have a participant or two who can recall a time when they were uncertain about their next breath of air. Once upon a time, they had their oxygen supply cut off.

If you had your oxygen cut off, I am willing to bet you would be focused on getting that next breath of air! Every thought and fiber of your being would do all you could to get another breath before you breathe your last. Thankfully, apparently all my participants have successfully continued to get all the air they need or they would be somewhere else (certain of what happens next)!

You need air or you die. Let me ask you a question. Have you once worried about your next breath of air at any point today? How about right now? If you don't get a breath by the end of the next few paragraphs, you will be dead. And you aren't concerned.

That's because your need for oxygen is being met so you are O.K.! If your need suddenly isn't met, that need becomes the most important thing in your life. But once the need is met, you can focus on other needs, one of which is *now* the most important unsatisfied need. The cycle continues with your need for food and water. Procreation probably fits in as a basic physical need, and that alone explains a lot of human behavior.

SECURITY NEEDS

The next level of needs address your future, your plans for your next meal, where you will sleep, how to protect your stuff, and pay your bills. No wonder people get so passionate about their guns! An arsenal of weapons satisfies some folks' basic human need for security. Like food and air, once security needs are satisfied, you are on to the next higher level of needs.

SOCIAL NEEDS

Well-fed and well-armed, you reach out to your neighbor; you throw a party; you join a group; you put a decal on your car identifying your membership in a group; you become part of something bigger and more powerful than yourself. You satisfy your social needs because loneliness isn't much fun.

SELF-ESTEEM NEEDS

Finally, you get an opportunity to do something that makes you feel good about yourself. You go to the gym; you run around your neighborhood; you volunteer your time; you organize fundraisers; you take a class; you enter a competition; you win a trophy; you get applause; you feel O.K.!

Here is the hierarchy so far:

Self-Esteem
Social
Security
Physical

Remember, only when a lower level need is met will the higher need serve as a motivator. Until that need is met, the higher needs fail to motivate. No wonder it is so hard to exercise for 30 minutes every day. You have to go to work to earn the money that pays the rent. You need to live in a safe and secure neighborhood and buy groceries to feed the hungry faces that your physical, social, and self-esteem needs brought into your dining room. Then you have even more procreation and social needs which have to be met before you are even tempted to do anything that feels good—like go out for a 30-minute run around the neighborhood.

Only when that host of needs is met can you focus your energies on the final remaining need in the hierarchy.

Remember the appeal the U.S. Army used a few years ago to get young Americans to join the Army? Recruiting soldiers always appeared, to me, to be a tough sell—motivating young civilians to join that particular organization. The U.S. Army came up with a nifty answer and a swell tune to accompany the answer to the question: Why join the U.S. Army? So that you can "Be all that you can be…!" You can probably sing the answer to why right along with your Army recruiter. The recruiter is making an appeal to the highest level of Maslow's hierarchy.

SELF-ACTUALIZATION NEEDS

The need to reach your human potential is the need to be all that you can be. Maslow called this self-actualization. You get in the best shape of your life; you finish your college education; you make important differences in your community; you find all the answers to true happiness!

Unfortunately, first you have to eat, go to work, pay taxes, go on a date, and watch some TV. Then you will be ready.

The U.S. Army does what all great motivators do. They appeal to all of the human needs at the same time. Remember, before you can self-actualize, you have other fundamentally more important needs—like surviving until tomorrow.

The U.S. Army assures a recruit that you will never have to worry about where your next meal is coming from or where you are going to rest your pretty little head at night if you join our group. Plus, you will never again be lonely, and you will have a platoon of terrific new friends starting with Drill Sgt. Carter. Then we will get you in the best shape of your life. You can feel terrific about yourself as you wear the uniform of the greatest army in the history of mankind. You will receive an opportunity to be a hero. Then, when it is all over with, we will give you money toward your college education so that you can be all that you can be.

Now then, if your audience is hungry, insecure, lonely, not sure if they are O.K., and has no clue how to go about achieving their human potential, then you need to convince them that cooperating with you will satisfy their needs. The Army makes an offer their target audience can't refuse. Some folks will do just about anything if you give them what they want: food, shelter, companionship, approval, and achievement. All felt needs. You feel hungry; you feel insecure; you feel lonely; you feel inadequate.

This is a popular theory, but Maslow has his critics. One criticism is that this is a circular explanation. The question of motivation is always answered with: Because he felt like it. The theory is circular because the answer is always the same regardless of the observation.

The other criticism is what the theory says about you and me. Uncertainty Reduction is the theory that suggests we do things because we are curious. Maslow's Hierarchy Theory suggests you and I are needy. We feel a need and we act. This theory is criticized because it says you and I are selfish, egocentric, needy little things who are motivated to satisfy our own personal needs; we look out for number one; it is our needs that demand satisfaction.

The theory suggests that the way to ensure cooperation is to satisfy your audience's selfish needs. That sounds familiar and it makes sense.

But there is also the altruistic motive in the human experience. There are those among us whose behavior is best explained by their need to serve the needs of their neighbor. There are some who serve our militaries and police departments because they want a chance to protect the best interests of others. There are some who work hard to offer support and encouragement to others, and there are some who make a special effort to assure everyone they are O.K. just the way they are! There are some Americans that do what they do for little recognition, little appreciation, and little pay because their job gives them a chance to serve the needs of others.

For some, that *is* being all that you can be.

Schutz's Interpersonal Needs Theory

Of all the theories that seek to explain human behavior, I believe the most practical explanation I share with my students is William B. Schutz's Interpersonal Needs Theory. Instead of basic human needs, this theory emphasizes the interpersonal needs of humans. This theory is an example of a balance theory.

Schutz's Theory is similar to Maslow's in that it, too, suggests there are things we selfishly need satisfied. However, this theory recognizes there is also the altruistic motive. We feel a need to give to others just as we have a need to get from others. What is it we want to get from others, and what is it we want to give to others?

It is the Same Thing

This is an important point in understanding human motivation. What we want to get are the same things that we want to give. What we all want to get and what we all want to give are: Control, Inclusion, and Approval.

This theory suggests that all of us have the need for control: the need to do what you want, when you want, how you want, with whom you want, and where you want. Liberty and freedom are reflections of our fundamental need for control. While all of us have that need, some of us have a very high need for control. We call these people control freaks. They want to control everything and everyone. They want to be in charge; they want to issue orders; they want to be in command of all they survey.

Control freaks have a very HIGH need to control others, to EXPRESS control. However, they do not like being told what to do, do not like threats to their authority, and have a very LOW need to RECEIVE control from other people.

The same is true of the other needs in Schutz's Theory of Interpersonal Needs. Some of us have a HIGH need for Inclusion, and others of us don't join groups, avoid team efforts, and prefer quiet time alone.

Some of us have a very HIGH need to RECEIVE Approval from others, and others of us don't care what people think about us. Those of us who have a very high need for approval may actually be secretly jealous of those people who can easily march through life with no concern for what others think. A former colleague had a name for this envy. He called it A****** Envy. The reason we might tolerate and even admire the most boorish and inconsiderate behavior is that we wish we could act like an a******. Some people take pride in the fact they don't care what others may think. Fortunately, most of us have a greater need for approval that prevents us from doing what we want, when we want to do it, with whom we want, and where we want do it, say it, or display it. Most of us care about our image, identity, and what others might think of us.

Military Application

The U.S. Navy had a problem. Sometimes, you ask a group of individuals to function as a military unit, and they do it. Each member of the unit subordinates their selfish, egocentric, and personal needs in favor of the needs of the unit. In fact, the expectation is that each member of that unit would be willing to make the supreme sacrifice for the mission and "take a bullet" for any member of the unit.

Sometimes it works that way and sometimes it doesn't. That is a problem for a military unit. "Take a bullet for you? No way, I am using you as a shield!" How can you predict which groups of individuals are going to function as a unit and which units will function as a group of separate individuals? Schutz offered the Navy an explanation.

Let's say the Navy randomly selects a group of five individuals of equal rank to function as a military unit. Unfortunately, each of these individuals selected have a very HIGH need to EXPRESS CONTROL. Can we predict how this team is going to function? You bet. The first time one of them barks an order to the others, his entire audience revolts, and each of the other four demands compliance from everyone else. "Too many Chiefs and not enough Indians" is the clichéd observation of these conflicts over control.

Let's say they select another group of four to complete the mission the previous five failed to complete. Only this time, all four individuals have a very LOW need to EXPRESS CONTROL. The first day, one of them asks the other three, "What do you want to do?" The predictable response from the first would be, "I don't know. What do you want to do?"

The second says, "Don't look at me; I'm not in charge; I just take orders; I just do what I am told to do."

The third says, "Well, don't look to me. I don't want the responsibility, and I am not accountable for what happens!"

Now, let's say a fifth sailor who has a HIGH need to EXPRESS CONTROL steps up to say, "I am in charge here. You four take orders from me. I am in control of this mission, and I have all the answers. I will take care of all your needs, and you will obey my every command!" The message is: Give me what I want, and I will give you what you want.

Boot Camps and Police Academies are schools specifically designed to teach the art of taking an order. Lots of people need the discipline and need to learn how to function as a team. Academies also insist that recruits learn to follow an order before they are expected to give an order. Titles and ranks are used to avoid battles over control. Some of us are eager to take control. Some of us are happy to let others take control. Which are you?

YOU CAN TAKE A TEST

Schutz and his colleagues designed a test that will tell you the intensity of your interpersonal needs. The assessment is a set of 60 statements designed to measure the intensity of your six needs to EXPRESS and RECEIVE Control, Inclusion, and Approval.

The test has 60 statements. You are asked to agree or disagree with each statement related to one of the six needs. Ten statements are specific to each of the six needs suggested by the theory. If you agree with all ten statements related to your need to RECEIVE Inclusion, then you would score VERY HIGH on that interpersonal need. Let's say on your need to EXPRESS Approval to others you scored VERY LOW because you disagreed with most of the statements measuring that need. Later on the test, you agreed with five of the statements related to the need to RECEIVE Control from others, and disagreed with the other five statements. In that case, you would receive a MEDIUM score on that need.

I like this theory because it helps in our understanding of how to give difficult people what they want. Often, they simply want some control, to be included, and to hear that they are O.K.!

This theory helps in understanding our own personal motivations, needs, and behaviors. The theory also contributes to an understanding of the needs of the important people in our lives.

I took the test, and the results told me what I already knew about myself:

	RECEIVE	EXPRESS
CONTROL	Low	High
INCLUSION	High	Low
APPROVAL	Very High	Medium

The test told me that I am a control freak who can't take an order, who hates to be left behind but prefers to work alone, and who is, above all else, motivated by the approval of others. No one likes your applause more than I do!

I often ask my audiences if they knew only that I crave approval, what could they predict about the needs of the love of my life, Melissa? If you guessed that she has a HIGH need to EXPRESS approval to others, you guessed right. She is a trained and experienced kindergarten teacher. She delights in the opportunity to take five year-old little boys into her arms, rub their heads, and say, "Bless your heart, you wonderful thing!"

Thirty years ago, I decided that I needed a lot of that, and so I married her over 24 years ago. I have been delighted to get what I want all these years. And a few years ago, I convinced her to work with me as my only partner in my seminar business. I needed the help, and I needed her around to rub my head and tell me that it was all going to be O.K.!

I have also learned if you want the approval of others, then you better not march through life criticizing, condemning, and complaining about the important people in your life. The other thing about me is that I am something of a control freak. I like being in charge; I like being a professional speaker; I liked being a professor. Great job if you are a control freak, a lot like being a cop I suppose. You issue commands; you demand respect; you punish the misbehavers; you evaluate; you assess; you have all the answers; you alone tell your audience what is going to happen next and when they are dismissed. Sounds a lot like a kindergarten teacher's job as well.

I wasn't always a happy man. I wasn't always in as much control as I desired. Just after my high school graduation in May of 1976, I was inducted into the Air Force Academy as an Air Force cadet. The appointment is competitive, and it delighted my Dad, a career Air Force pilot, to see his son attend the military academy. I am sure he was also delighted it was a tuition-free education with a guaranteed job for me as a military officer after graduation.

With no other similar offers, I had little choice but to accept the appointment and begin boot camp at the Air Force Academy during the summer of 1976.

I had made it about two, maybe three weeks when I came up with a number of suggestions that might better satisfy my needs at the Air Force Academy in general but specifically about the treatment of basic recruits at their Summer Boot Camp. Being something of a control freak, I resented the fact I had very little choice about a number of things in the military: haircuts, uniforms, bedtime, when I got up, what I ate, where I ate it, how I ate it, and who I ate it with. I was given little choice in where I showered, how long I showered, and who I showered with. After a few weeks of Boot Camp, I came up with a number of suggestions related to how the Air Force Academy could do a better job of accommodating MY needs. I had learned that although I like to be in charge, I do not like to take orders, and I prefer to have a choice as often as possible.

Predictably, the Air Force Academy refused to change to satisfy my needs, and the officers suggested maybe I should find a change of career and address.

They shipped me back to Fort Worth to my parents. My less than delighted Dad began paying my tuition at Texas Christian University. That September, I enrolled in a Basic Public Speaking class. In that classroom, I found my true calling. I wanted to help others do a better job of presenting their messages in public. Sitting in that classroom, I decided I wanted that professor's job. That job looked like one I could be happy doing. Three degrees later and you know the rest of the story.

I enjoyed the control of being in charge of a classroom; I love the control I have now as an entrepreneur and professional speaker. And let me tell you another thing about this control freak. I live with three women, and I enjoy complete control over every aspect of my household and complete control over every aspect my wife's and two daughters' lives. I am the king of my castle; I am The Man; I wear the pants in my house; I rule; I am in total control!

I sense your skepticism. I see it in my audience's faces every time I make those claims. Let me assure you what I claim is the way things really are!

For example, just last Sunday when I was fixing breakfast for my family, I asked Melissa for her permission to make each of the claims above. "Of course, you are The Man, the king of your castle, and you make every decision. Feel free to make that claim to anyone, anywhere, at anytime."

"Then I have your permission?" I asked.

"You have my permission," was her reply.

So, there you go! I trust your skepticism has now abated.

WHO IS REALLY IN CONTROL?

Now then, if all of the above was true, who is actually in charge of my household? Well, you know who isn't in control. But my wife is something of a social genius, and she has successfully managed a control freak for 30 years. She knows the easiest way to deal with a difficult person is to let them think they are getting what they want. She lets me see things as I prefer to see them.

She applied this understanding even before breakfast last Sunday. Just as I got out of bed, eager to get to the golf course, Melissa came rushing into our bedroom and said, "Brian, you have to make a decision. Since you are the decision-maker of this family, I came directly to you for your direction and advice. I will do as you command."

Happy to fulfill my manly duties before I rushed off to the golf course, I asked, "What is the nature of the decision I must make?"

She explained, "One of us is cooking breakfast and one of us is doing laundry. You must decide which one you are going to do."

"Since I am the superior cook, I shall cook our morning meal and you shall do my laundry!" I commanded.

"As you wish my king," she said as I marched upstairs, put on my apron, and fixed breakfast.

Professional law enforcement officers apply the same understanding of control when they tell a suspect, "Look, we can do this the hard way or the easy way. You are in charge; you are the Boss; you tell me which way it is going to be."

If your audience has a HIGH need for control, by giving them a choice you give them control. My wife and great cops know that to get control you have to give control by offering options and a choice. He who controls the options controls the outcome. Just make your audience an offer they can't refuse!

WHY ARE YOU SO ANGRY?

I find this theory helps me understand my options for giving people what they want. Because when people don't get what they want, they become difficult. Angry people are angry because they aren't getting what they want. Think about the last time you got angry. If you said, "I can't get these idiots to do what I want," you were angry because your control needs weren't being met. If, instead, you said, "I never know what's going on around here. I am always the last one to hear about anything," then your inclusion needs have been violated. Finally, if you angrily said, "Man, no one ever appreciates the hard work I do," then you are mad because your needs for approval aren't being met.

Schutz's theory also helps us understand the motives of others. Many of my seminar participants are familiar with the HBO documentary *Gang Banging in Little Rock*. The program shows the violence associated with urban gangs.

The film leaves many wondering why any urban youth would want to join a gang? The initiation is violent; the life style is dangerous; the life span of a gang member on the streets is often brief. Why would someone want to join an urban gang?

Schutz has an answer: Control, Inclusion, and Approval. The gang gives its members what they want and need: Control in the form of how to dress, where to stand, and what to do; Inclusion in something bigger and more powerful; and Approval because they have a whole gang telling them that they are O.K.!

How does a community combat the problem of urban gangs? Give urban youth what they want so they don't need a gang to satisfy their needs. I recently worked with the North Little Police Department and learned what they do to address their city's gang problem. One program is remarkably simple and exceptionally effective. The city provides year-round athletic programs in baseball, tennis, martial arts, football, and basketball. The police recruit, initiate, and coach teams of urban youths. With a ball in their hand, it is difficult to pick up a gun. The police keep a ball in their hand as often as possible to remarkable effect.

The rewards are many. Mentors offer guidance, rules to follow, social groups, competition, and trophies. Other education programs focus on inner city four and five year-olds to ensure they get a proper start on an education that provides options, choice, and control over an uncertain future. The lessons they learn early in life are often the most important lessons. The teachers, officers, and important people in these young lives are demonstrating how to be an important person.

Occasionally, you are a difficult person. Often, you are difficult because you aren't getting what you want. You probably wanted to have a choice, to be informed, and to be appreciated. Melissa's aunt said many years ago, after babysitting the five year-old who would enter my life a decade later, "She is easy to get along with just as long as you give her what she wants!"

CHAPTER NINE REVIEW:
WHY DO PEOPLE DO WHAT THEY DO?

The three theories in this chapter provide a basic understanding of human behavior.

Uncertainty reduction is a powerful motivator.

Certainty provides prediction, and with prediction comes control, and with control we get what we want!

We are uncomfortable with uncertainty.

We prefer to think we have all the answers.

Maslow's Hierarchy of Needs suggests a set of lower needs must be met before the higher needs serve to motivate:
- ❑ *Self-Actualization*
- ❑ *Self-Esteem*
- ❑ *Social Needs*
- ❑ *Security Needs*
- ❑ *Physiological Needs*

Motivational efforts often appeal to a wide variety of needs.

The human experience includes both selfish and altruistic motives for behavior.

Schutz's Interpersonal Needs Theory explains behavior as a response to needs for *Control, Inclusion, and Approval.*

Interpersonal Needs Theory includes both the need to express and receive: *Control, Inclusion, and Approval.*

The six Interpersonal Needs may be expressed by predictable behaviors, and the depth of each need can vary across and within individuals.

Often you have to give in order to receive:
- ❑ *You get control by giving choices.*
- ❑ *You get included by including others in your life.*
- ❑ *You get approval by expressing approval.*

TEN
Developing
Communication Plans

Professional law enforcement officers have a distinct advantage when they have a prepared verbal plan for responding appropriately and professionally. Many of my lectures, in university classrooms and professional development seminars, focus on developing communication plans. In fact, I had long believed that once I got around to writing my book, the title would be *Communication Plans*.

Then, several years ago, I found a book on the shelves of my local bookstore with the title: *LifeScripts, What To Say To Get What You Want in 101 of Life's Toughest Situations*. Holding the book in my hand, I was reminded of what my University of Kansas professor had advised me years before, "Polansky, anytime that you think you have come up with something novel or original to write, it only means you haven't read enough."

I purchased the book by Stephen Pollan and Mark Levine. I scanned the 101 tough situations and saw a verbal plan for getting a raise in pay, negotiating a lower credit card interest rate, returning food at a restaurant, and handling a sexual harassment complaint. I recall tough situation #99 was "Breaking a Wedding Engagement," and #101 of life's toughest situations was "Asking Your Spouse to Lose Weight." Now, most of you wouldn't dream of trying, but if you wanted a script for trying, *LifeScripts* has a verbal plan for getting your spouse to lose weight.

As I thumbed through the pages, I realized I was already teaching this subject. I had been teaching the process of developing appropriate and effective communication plans in my interpersonal and business communication courses for years. The central features of a public speaking course are the development of an outline, extensive research, and rehearsal before opening your mouth in front of an audience. My lectures on conflict management, interpersonal relationships, persuasive speaking, and negotiation all focus on the development of effective communication plans. I was curious how much of what I had been teaching for decades was in the pages of *LifeScripts*.

I found my old professor was correct. I found it was all in the book. It became clear that the ten principles I share in a 30-minute lecture on "Communication Plans" are imbedded throughout the verbal plans for 101 of life's toughest situations. My audiences are delighted to learn that only ten universal principles of persuasive interaction will prepare them for not only 101 but also for 10,001 of life's most difficult situations. By embracing just a few principles of human interaction, each of us can become more successful in our efforts to find the right words to say at the right time to get the right people to do the right thing.

IDENTIFY YOUR TRUE GOAL

What do you want? What are your short-term and long-term objectives? How do you want to be perceived? How do you want your audience to feel? What exactly do you want to happen first? Are your intentions altruistic or self-serving? Are you hoping to win a battle or win the war? Do you want truth, justice, control, inclusion, approval, security, status, respect, revenge, recognition, regrets, remorse, reassurance, an admission, an apology, a bargain, a voice, a choice, and/or is it just a bigger piece of Mom's apple pie? In public speaking, students are advised to first develop a specific purpose that defines the presentation's true goal.

Notice I emphasize TRUE goal. It is important to define exactly what your goal is because sometimes what we ask for is only a symptom of what we should *really* be asking for.

Let's look at the 101st of life's toughest situations: Getting your spouse to lose weight. If I ask most folks, "What is your true goal in this situation?" Many will answer, "Well, it is obvious: Getting your spouse to lose weight!" Other participants make an effort at identifying the true goal by pointing out the benefits of losing weight. No one ever gives me the answer I am looking for. So, I then ask the question this way: "If someone is going to lose weight, what two things are they going to have to do?"

"Diet and exercise," most of my participants correctly answer. Some still argue, "No, first they have to *want to* lose weight." I point out that even if you didn't want to lose weight but you started taking in fewer calories than you burned up, you would lose weight. Just ask my Uncle Bob, the stomach cancer patient.

With the true goal of getting your spouse to diet and exercise, finding the right words suddenly becomes a lot easier. The same principle applies in all of the other 10,001 of life's difficult situations.

LOOK TO THE FUTURE AND AVOID THE PAST

When someone suggests we are NOT O.K., how many of us ask, "Well then, how can I change?" How many of us ask in the hopes of avoiding this conversation in the future?

I fear most of us get combative rather than cooperative. Some of us are tempted to point out occasions, in the past, where our accusers were NOT O.K. and retort, "How about last week when you...and remember Thanksgiving when you and your mother and your whole damn family did the same thing only worse?"

We spoke in Chapter Three about the critical difference between these questions:

"Let me ask you, WHY are you..."

"Let me ask you, HOW can I..."

The former question is looking to the past for an explanation; the latter is clearly a forward-looking question that looks to the future and avoids the past.

Most difficult situations are difficult because it is difficult to answer questions of WHY? Successful communication plans emphasize HOW things need to be.

Imagine a scene where a wife steps in front of the TV her husband is watching and says, "Let me ask you a question, honey?"

She then turns her backside to him, bends over, and asks, "Do these new jeans make my butt look big?" In a recent seminar with North Little Rock police officers, a voice in the back boomed, "Heck no, Darling! It is your fat ass making those jeans look too small!" I did a quick check to confirm it was, indeed, the officer who had earlier admitted to four marriages in the past 20 years.

CHOOSE A PROPER ATTITUDE TO PROJECT

There are almost a million words in the English language. No wonder it is difficult to find the right words when you have a million to choose from. But as soon as you settle on an appropriate attitude for your communication plan, your word choice becomes severely limited. You can only use the few words (and the tone and style of delivery) that support the appropriate attitude you plan to maintain throughout your persuasive interaction.

Exactly what attitude do you want to project through your communication plan? Do you want to project an attitude seething with resentment, anger, frustration, or condemnation? Possibly, you would prefer to be seen as professional, concerned, humble, embarrassed, apologetic, agreeable, friendly, hopeful, or helpful.

There is a universal attitude that is appropriate for almost any difficult situation. The Universal Attitude is: I've Got Your Best Interest At Heart! There are few situations where the clear demonstration of an altruistic motive isn't appropriate. The majority of your plans for getting cooperation will often be devoted to making it clear that cooperation is in your audience's best interest. Whether the goal is to get proper service at a restaurant or to secure a confession to a capital murder, the attitude is the same.

Could you use this attitude to break a wedding engagement? You bet you could because it is in no one's best interest to be in a loveless marriage.

START FROM A POSITION OF SERVICE

As a professional speaker, I hope my audiences see me as confident and comfortable. I try to project confidence when I speak to any audience. I trust that occasionally I have an audience member listen to my presentation and say to themselves, "By golly, that Polansky sure is a comfortable and confident public speaker! I wonder what his secret is? Why is he so very comfortable speaking to this large group of professionals?"

I'll share my secret with you. The armor I put on, the armor that protects me from any self-doubt and discomfort while presenting to any audience is a verbal armor of words. With every audience I speak to and in every presentation I give, I always start with the same words:

"Please allow me to introduce myself. My name is Brian. I'm a doctor and I'm here to help you."

I can personally assure you if your true goal is to help other people, there is not a room that you cannot comfortably step into with confidence and find the right words to say. You can even find enough words to fill up a two-day seminar, and you can find the words to fill a book if you are motivated to try to help other people.

Focus on the Behavior, Not the Person

HOUSEGUESTS AND FISH

When I travel to Fort Worth, I stay at the house of a long-time friend from high school who is single and lives alone. We enjoy each other's company, and we both look forward to my visits back home. Since Jeff is single and doesn't travel, he is always available, but I have a key to his place just in case. I get the best benefits, a free room and great companionship. Jeff is one of the few people still in my life who I have known longer than Melissa. His place is my home away from home when I am working anywhere in North Texas.

Recently, I had a long stretch of work in Fort Worth and stayed at my good friend's house for most of a week. During my stay, I was reminded of the old saying "houseguests and fish both begin to stink after three days." One night, we were cleaning up in Jeff's kitchen while steaks cooked outside on the grill. When Jeff saw the mess I had left on his counter while I was seasoning the steaks, the resentment of all the little messes of mine he had been silently cleaning and tallying over the past few days came pouring out in a verbal torrent of hostility I rarely encounter. "YOU ARE A SLOB! Look at all this salt and pepper on the counter. You are a damn SLOB! You leave toothpaste in the sink; you drop your towels on the floor; you don't shut the shower curtain; you leave every light on in the house; you leave your crap everywhere. You are worse than my kids. YOU ARE A SLOB!" he screamed in my shell-shocked face.

> I could not disagree. I am a slob. My office is a mess, my garage is a mess, and my closet is a mess. I live with people who tolerate and pick up after me. When I stay alone at a hotel, I pretty much dump everything on the floor first thing after arrival, throw wet towels on the bathroom floor, and never really pick up after myself. I realized I was so comfortable at Jeff's place I was acting like I was at home!

****

After my host's tirade, I briefly got my feelings hurt, started to pick up all my stuff and move to a hotel down the road. Then Jeff's angry and frustrated words reminded me that I had forgotten to include this principle in this chapter: Focus on the behavior, not the person.

As you develop your communication plans, remember there is a big difference between saying,

"You are a LIAR!" and
"When you say things that later prove to be untrue…"

"You are a BACKSTABBER!" and
"When you say that about me behind my back…"

"You are a THIEF!" and
"When you take my things without my permission…"

"You are a SLOB!" and
"When you don't pick up your wet towels…"

No one wants to be told they are not O.K., but it becomes difficult to avoid when we are in a position of policing other's behavior. The trick is to assure others that THEY are O.K. it is just that their behavior isn't.

ACKNOWLEDGE VIEWPOINTS

Many of life's most difficult situations are actually mini-counseling sessions. Consequently, the principles used by counseling psychologists are helpful to apply in many of our personal situations. You will recall from Chapter Five the first principle of the helping conversation:

Acknowledge the opinions and feelings of others as valid.

Reassure others that their feelings are valid, and that it is O.K. to feel the way they are feeling. You might say something like, "You have every right to be angry, Jeff. I have taken advantage of your hospitality. I am sure your frustration has been justifiably building. You are right. I am a slob, but I will change. I'll make it up to you by cleaning up after myself. Thank you for sharing your true feelings with me, and I'll tell you what I'm going to do for you. I am taking full responsibility for cleaning up after tonight's meal. Jeff, is there anything else I can do to help you out?"

ANTICIPATE OBJECTIONS

For years, I taught an advanced public speaking class which included student debates. I taught my debaters to always anticipate their opponent's arguments. I suggested each student consider employing a strategy of refutation. The key to the strategy is to refute your opponent's arguments before they can use them.

Most college students, when assigned a persuasive speech on a controversial topic, would organize their outline in a statement of reasons. The first main point is the student's first good reason why they support their side of the proposition. The second point is their second reason why and so on.

Occasionally, a rare student would employ a strategy of refutation. The speaker would step to the podium and say, "I am not going to argue why you should support my proposition in favor of this issue. Today, I am going to refute each of my opponent's arguments why you should not support it. My opponent claims the proposition is too costly; there is not enough time to do what I ask; there is no proof the proposition will make a true difference. I will prove none of my opponent's objections are valid reasons not to support my proposition. Therefore, you must support my proposition."

Our primary objection to cooperation is the belief that compliance is not in our best interest. Persuasive interaction endeavors to change that perception. Beyond self-interest, the most common objections are the three listed above: cost, time, and a positive outcome.

I am a professional speaker, and I need organizations to hire me so I can pay my daughters' bills. Many may object to cooperating with me, citing the fees I charge are too expensive, their schedules don't allow for a full-day seminar, or the training might be a waste of time.

If I can refute the arguments of cost, time, and impact of the training, then I will be more successful in getting cooperation from potential clients and paying my bills. If you want your spouse to diet and exercise, you may need to refute his or her current beliefs and argue that a healthier lifestyle would be in his or her best interest, save money, take little time, and would absolutely reap positive and immediate benefits.

Ask for Their Assistance

What is the quickest, easiest way to make someone feel important? ASK for their help! You want more cooperation from your young son? Make his cooperation make him feel important—that those chores are important jobs, ones that make important differences, and are done by important people. How does Lincoln fire a general and allow his officer to save face? By asking the general for help with an important problem.

When we were young parents, my wife would ask Lauren for help with her infant sister. Melissa would repeatedly remind Lauren of how important she is and the important help she provides. My now 21 year-old daughter allowed last week that her 16 year-old sister is her best friend and figures it will always be that way. This pleased both Melissa and me to no end, but it didn't surprise me. Recently, I was looking at old videos of when my daughters were young. In one tape, there is footage of five year-old Lauren saying to her baby sister, "You are a lucky baby because you have a really nice big sister to help you out!" Where do you suppose she got that idea, and what do you suppose are the consequences of believing you are an important person to someone?

Could you use this principle for the tough goal of getting your spouse to diet and exercise? You bet. The strategy would sound like this. "Darling, I need some help. I am starting a new diet and exercise program, but I fear I will fail without your help. I have started and failed dozens of fitness efforts in the past. I need some help if I am going to succeed this time. Will you help me? Can I ask that we start going for walks after dinner together? Will you join me on this new diet program? I am only asking because with your help I believe I can succeed."

Helping people makes people feel important. I still occasionally have to re-learn this lesson and how it applies in persuasive interaction.

THE DALLAS STRATEGY

Once when traveling from Austin to Little Rock through DFW airport, I decided to change my plans. Instead of traveling on the second leg of my scheduled flight back home to Little Rock, I decided, at the last minute, I would simply get off in Dallas and visit my family in Fort Worth for the weekend. I had seminars planned for the next week in North Texas, so it looked like a good chance to visit my 84 year-old mother. I called Mama and told her the good news, and I called my brother to pick me up at DFW. He said he would be delighted and added, "Mom is getting old; she will enjoy the visit; she isn't going to be around for much longer!"

Upon checking in at Austin Airport, I was assured by a baggage handler that although I was ticketed to Little Rock, I could retrieve my bags at DFW. He said, "Just tell them at your gate upstairs, and the attendant will take care of it." So, I checked my bags.

Prior to boarding, I asked the flight attendant at the gate to make sure my bags got off with me in Dallas. In no uncertain terms, she informed me my bags were going to Little Rock, that FAA regulations require bags to go where ticketed, and to take it up with a supervisor at check-in. I frantically ran back down to check-in and was told, "Your bags are going to Little Rock, as ticketed, unless you want to purchase another one-way ticket to DFW for your bags."

I argued, "Look, your personnel told me I could get my bags. I am a frequent flyer, I am an important person, I do important things, I have important work next week, and I need my bags when I get off in Dallas!"

The supervisor said, "Nothing I can do, following policy, your bags are going to Little Rock, and you better hurry if you are going to make your flight, or you will need to purchase another ticket!"

Exasperated, I rushed back to the gate and arrived just in time to board my flight and buckle in next to an unfortunate stranger. I complained to my seatmate the entire flight about how I was wronged, about how my Mama was going to be disappointed, that my brother was waiting, and I didn't know what to do because I couldn't stay in Texas if my luggage went on to Little Rock.

It was only a 50-minute flight but just enough time to see the error of my ways and to form a new plan. In Dallas, I exited the plane and sprinted straight to the gate for the flight to Little Rock.

I rushed breathlessly to the gate, approached the ticket counter, and heaved a long, mournful sigh. "Can I help you?" the agent at the desk asked the pitiful sight of a man at wits end.

"Gosh, I sure hope so. I could really use some help right now. I am scheduled to get on that plane to Little Rock, but I just received some awful news, and I am going to have to stay here in Dallas a few days. My brother should be waiting for me outside right now. I need some help!"

The concerned agent said, "So, you want me to cancel your flight to Little Rock?"

"Yes, that would be a great deal of help. Thanks, cancel the flight."

"Done. Is there anything else I can do to help you, sir?"

"Yes you can. I decided to cancel that flight only after I spoke to my brother. The awful news is my brother is convinced my mother doesn't have long to live, and he is parked outside to whisk me to her side for possibly the last time."

"I am so sorry. Sir, how can I help?"

"My two bags are being loaded onto that plane bound for Little Rock, and I need them before I meet my brother. Can you help me?"

"Give me five minutes!" she said as she disappeared around the corner.

Five minutes later, with more than a little guilt, I had my bags in hand. And, after my visit, my mom pulled through!

****

The error of my previous strategy was expecting to get service because I was an important person. The Dallas Strategy was to get cooperation by making someone else an important person. (FYI: my mom was 84 years old, had recently suffered a broken hip, was in the hospital, and my brother had, that day, encouraged me to find a way to spend some time with her before it was too late.)

I hear from many participants who have used the Dallas Strategy to get immediate cooperation from appliance salesmen, cell phone companies, garage mechanics, and many others by starting with, "Can you help me?"

Politely Ask for What You Want

I bought *LifeScripts* because I was also hoping to find support in the book for my argument that your most important verbal skill is asking questions. I found my support because all 101 of the scripts for life's toughest situations made specific use of simply asking for what you want. Consistently, the attitude is "Hey, I'm just asking!"

Many of my participant's have credit card debt. I trust some are paying a much higher credit card interest rate than they have to. To those I ask, "If you want your credit card company to give you a lower interest rate on your purchases, what do you need to do?" Ask!

The principle: *you get what you ask for* is never more certain than in the marketplace. If you don't ask, they are never going to give it to you! So, ask away.

I have, over the years, become much better at asking for what I want when I am on the road: hotel upgrades, special discounts, fee waivers, complimentary meals, and late checkouts.

Students were often eager to learn how they can talk their way out of a traffic ticket. I suggest, "Admit your guilt, express remorse, and then respectfully ASK for a warning."

I use this strategy at home also. "Girls, I need some help. Can I ask…" begins a lot of conversations in my home.

STATE BENEFITS OF COOPERATION

If what you are asking for is in your audience's best interest, then listing the benefits of cooperation should be easy. Answer the obvious question on the minds of your audience: What is in it for me? If you cannot cite any audience benefit, maybe you should reconsider the request.

I read a frightening statistic recently in *USA Today*. The current generation of children is the first generation of Americans who scientists expect to have a shorter life span than their parents. Why? The article states we have more obese kids than ever. Obese kids today forecasts a future population of adults with diabetes, heart disease, depression, and consequent expectations of much shorter lives. Maybe it is not their own waistline parents should be worried about. Maybe the entire family could benefit from 30 minutes of vigorous daily activity and fewer super-sized meals.

Summary of Principles

The ten principles that will guide you in your efforts to say the right thing in 10,001 of life's most difficult situations:

Determine Your True Goal
Look to the Future and Avoid the Past
Choose an Appropriate Attitude to Project
Start from a Position of Service
Focus on the Behavior, Not the Person
Acknowledge Other's Views and Feelings as Valid
Anticipate Objections to Cooperation
Consider Asking for the Assistance of Others
Politely Ask for What You Want
State Benefits of Cooperation

Consider This

Consider a current situation in your life where the ten principles might help you find the right words:

1.

2.

3.

4.

5.

6.

7.

8.

9.

10.

A.E.I.O.U. MODEL OF STRATEGIC INTERACTION

If remembering ten principles is too difficult, let me offer you a five-step communication plan suggested by J. Wisinski in the book *Resolving Conflicts on the Job.* The five steps for getting others to cooperate with your requests are easy to remember: A.E.I.O.U.

Do you recall my story about the university administrator who was insistent on enrolling in my advanced public speaking class? You may recall her name was Diane, and you may recall I asked for an appointment and rushed over to the administration building. Before I swung open the door, I asked myself, "What is your communication plan here, Professor?"

Standing in the hot August sun, I needed a communication plan, quick! The five-step strategy I pulled from my mental archives was A.E.I.O.U. Here is how the strategy played out in my boss's, boss's, boss's assistant's office.

Step One:
ASSUME they mean well.
I am very impressed with your interest and willingness to enroll in a public speaking course. (Implicit: You are O.K.)

Step Two:
EXPRESS your concerns about their good intentions.
However, I am not so sure you are going to get what you think you are going to get out of that 15-week course.

Step Three:
INDICATE what you would like to have happen.
I am certain I can best serve your needs by serving as your speech coach and evaluating your campus presentations.

Step Four:
OUTCOME expected.
I'll make you a better speaker in two or three sessions instead of 15 weeks with novice college students.

Step Five:
UNDERSTAND on a mutual level.
Can we reach an understanding that you will let me serve as your coach, and you will quit showing up in my classroom?

That is it: A.E.I.O.U.

You may also recall Diane said, "Now, *that* is exactly what I am looking for!"

I said, "Then I will eagerly await your call!"

The rest of the story is I went back and waited in my office for a call from Diane. And I waited, and waited, and waited. I concluded the best thing that could possibly happen was going to actually happen. She NEVER called. Talk about your WIN-WIN outcome!

Then I asked myself, "Why not?" I think the answer to this question begins with answering exactly WHY she was in my classroom in the first place? You may recall it was her supervisor who strongly recommended Diane seek out some public speaking training. I don't believe she thought she needed training, possibly resented the suggestion, and was seeking an easy way out.

I suspect she accurately assessed the course with college students was going to be an easy skate for an experienced speaker. I also suspect Diane's goal was to do only as directed with as little effort and benefit as possible, so the next time her supervisor asked if she is getting the recommended training she could truthfully say, "Yes sir, I did exactly what you told me to do."

Win-Win for me though! I do not want students in my class because some supervisor ordered them in there. I do want true students of effective communication in my classroom, people like you who are reading this book. Thanks, you are O.K.!

THE REST OF THE VILLA STORY

There is a "rest of the story" to another of my favorite stories. Recall The Villa Story where I feigned deafness to handle a difficult situation with the pest control guy? Of course you do.

The rest of that story begins the first day of my last semester at the University. I stepped into one of my Communication 101 classrooms crowded with 35 students and said, "Good morning, I'm a doctor and I'm here to help you!" I saw I had three deaf students (two young men and a young woman) enrolled in my classroom because seated facing them was a translator signing my words.

I said to myself, "Well, I guess I'll skip The Villa Story this semester." As the semester progressed, I developed relationships with each of the three deaf students and their translator, Mr. West.

I found having Mr. West signing my words was a bit of a pain in my butt. Not because of him; he is O.K.! My problem was with my 32 students with perfect hearing. It seemed in the course of every lecture, I would use some of my great big professor words like "Aristotelian Rhetorical Appeals" or "etymologically speaking." I speak fast, and there are no short signs for some of these academic words. Poor Mr. West would occasionally be forced to frantically spell out some very long words. The problem for me was that my 32 hearing students would hear me use a big word and their heads would all turn to watch Mr. West frantically sign the big word. And it seemed whenever I would slip up and quote a colorful term or word in class, I would lose all eyes as all students would eagerly watch Mr. West demonstrate how to sign, "A******!"

I said to heck with it. I'm telling The Villa Story, deaf students or not. My rationale was they surely expect to be treated the same as all of my students. Plus, the story illustrates important future course material on Fight or Flight and coping with speaking anxiety. Finally, it was also my last semester at the University!

About the tenth week, we got to the chapter on conflict management. Traditionally, I open that lecture with The Villa Story. I took a deep breath before I stepped into the classroom and began. "Let me tell you a story that happened one summer session when I was teaching in this very class room…"

I told the story, got to the climax line, and said, "OU ARRAH GOWING TO HAD TO AUK SLOWAH." I continued, "I am deaf; you must slow down," in the same affected manner.

Now, predictably, the entire classroom erupted in laughter. After a moment, the students caught their breath, stifled their laughter, and I saw all 32 heads turn in the direction of the deaf students. I followed their stunned eyes to the deaf students and saw the three of them laughing hard but silently.

I marched over and spoke directly to the young co-ed so she could read my lips and asked, "Apparently my story didn't offend you, did it?"

She said, "Oh no, Dr. Polansky. I do that all the time!"

****

R.E.A.C.T. MODEL OF STRATEGIC INTERACTION

For years and years, I taught college students. Occasionally, I presented professional development seminars. Then I began teaching in the School of Law Enforcement Supervision. I found my presentations and content were easily adapted to just about any audience.

I was eventually asked to develop a course specifically for patrol officers on persuasive interaction. Although I was comfortable presenting my message to their supervisors, I was a bit intimidated by the prospect of making recommendations to officers on the front lines—officers working in environments in which saying the wrong thing at the wrong time to the wrong person could actually get you killed.

I threw myself into the literature and materials these officers receive in their academy and in-service police training on topics related to persuasive interaction. I filtered all of the new material through what I traditionally taught civilian audiences (the contents of this book) in the hopes of developing a much more directive strategy than the approach used in A.E.I.O.U. which often concludes with the final outcome uncertain. Patrol officers don't have the luxury of time and second opportunities to say the right thing. Difficult situations have to go in their favor the first time, every time.

I endeavored to develop a communication plan which, like A.E.I.O.U., was a simple five step verbal plan for law enforcement that concludes in the officer's certain favor. What I came up with is the Five Step R.E.A.C.T. Model of Strategic Interaction that would allow officers to quickly react with the right words that would both ensure officer safety and citizen compliance.

Although I developed R.E.A.C.T. for patrol officers, I share this verbal plan with each of my audiences. Turns out we all police behavior, and having a reliable verbal plan for encouraging cooperation seems to benefit everyone. You will also find these five steps are an efficient summary of what I teach on developing communication plans.

The first step is an application of my early lecture on what I believe to be your most important verbal skill. What is the quickest, simplest way to generate cooperation? ASK! But asking for cooperation is a particular question called making a request.

REQUEST

"Sir, may I please ask for your cooperation? Would you please step out of your vehicle for me? Ma'am, please step right over here by my partner. Now, I am going to ask that both of you ..."

Many an officer has gained entrance to a violator's home without the necessary search warrant by simply asking, "Sir, do you mind if we talk inside, please? Mind if I have a look around?"

"Sure, come on in. Have a look around," the soon regretful tenant says.

Many parents feel that in order to maintain discipline, control, and obedience they have to shout orders, commands, warnings, and threats in the manner of a Marine drill sergeant. Many of those parents would be surprised, as are some police officers, at the power of the simple request!

The ancient Greeks noted that when you make a request, your audience will respond in one of three ways. They will agree to cooperate. They will refuse to cooperate. Most likely, they will ask you a question. We could take time to review the likely question someone would ask a person requesting some cooperation. I trust that review isn't necessary. Let's move on to the second step of R.E.A.C.T.

EXPLAIN

You can wait for the inevitable questions, or you can anticipate the questions, "Why?" and "What is in it for me?"

Aristotle told his students to embrace the question WHY because if you can overcome the implied objection (cooperation is not in my best interest), you will get their cooperation because they are convinced it is in their best interest to comply.

Offer a logical and reasonable explanation as to why you are asking for their cooperation. A rational explanation will often satisfy even the most reluctant audience.

Officer: "Sir, may I ask that you please step out of your vehicle, and I'll tell you why I am asking. I observed your vehicle swerve across the centerline of the road twice in the last half-mile. I need to determine whether or not it is appropriate for you to be behind the wheel this evening. I need to ask you to step out, and please come to the rear of your vehicle and answer a couple of questions."

Seems like a reasonable request. I am not a cop, have never been a cop, never conducted a traffic stop, and never arrested anyone. When I was developing the R.E.A.C.T. Model, over a decade ago, the toughest behavior I had to police was getting my young daughter, Kendall, to go to bed at bedtime and stay in bed. Some nights, she repeatedly tested my patience. Late into the night, I would hear her tiny feet padding around upstairs. I could hear her snacking, watching TV, or visiting with the dog and cats after I had repeatedly insisted she stay in bed AND GO TO SLEEP!

Kendall was one of those kids who always wanted to know WHY and demanded an explanation for almost every request for cooperation. This was particularly frustrating for me because her big sister seemed to always do exactly what you asked without questioning why. (I often wonder where Kendall got her character traits. Where Kendall got the desire to be the smartest person in the room, an eagerness for athletic competition, to be strong-willed, logically inclined, and have a natural aversion to be told what to do is beyond me!)

Some nights, let's just say I'm glad there were no video cameras recording my every move as I attempted to generate compliance with my young daughter. It became clear I needed a communication plan.

As I was finishing the R.E.A.C.T. Model, I recognized that before I could recommend the five steps, I would have to field-test the verbal plan. Since I am not a cop, I couldn't try it on strangers on the street. However, I did have a particular "policing" problem at home I could test on a local citizen. One night, an opportunity presented itself.

Parent: "Kendall, I need your help, and I need it right now. Here is the problem you can help me with. Will you please tuck yourself in your bed upstairs tonight and go straight to sleep right now for me?"

Now, I could either wait for the inevitable, "WHY?" or I could jump right in with an explanation.

"It is past your bedtime. My request is important to you because you have a soccer tournament tomorrow in Searcy, so you will be getting up an hour earlier to make the drive north for your first game. Look, Kendall, you need a full night of rest if you are going to perform your best for your coach and your team. Your Mom and sister are already asleep. I ran 10 miles with the fellas today, and I can't carry you upstairs or fight with you over this. So, it is important to both of us, and I am just asking. Will you help me out tonight?

If Kendall were from the planet Vulcan, a logical explanation would satisfy her intellectual curiosity for an explanation as to WHY, and she would be in bed. Vulcans logically cooperate with a rational request. Unfortunately, we have to deal with red-blooded human beings. Humans have a tendency to sometimes not do the logical thing. Idiots, drunks, and young children often fail to grasp the logic and continue to insist, "Nope, ain't gonna cooperate!"

ALTERNATIVES

You asked, you explained, and asked again, and still you received zero cooperation. Do you suppose Aristotle would now suggest, "You asked nicely twice; now chop off their head."

No. Although your logic failed, you have another option. Next, try Pathos. Make an emotional appeal that will make them FEEL the need to cooperate by describing the unattractive alternative to not cooperating.

Parent: "Kendall, I asked for your cooperation and you refused. I then explained to you why your cooperation is important to both of us. Again, you refused. Now, let me describe your alternatives. If you do exactly as I request, I will be very grateful to my superstar soccer-playing daughter. In the morning, we are going to get up early and get in the car for the drive to Searcy for your games. Then, win or lose, we are going to stop at your favorite Mexican food restaurant on the north side of town and get those sopapillas you like so much.

BUT if I don't get your cooperation right now, and I mean RIGHT NOW, here is what is going to happen. I am going to reach down there, grab you by your pretty little wrist and march you up those stairs, bouncing your tender little rear end on each step along the way. Then we are going to get to the top of the steps, and you are going to do that flopping thing you do on the floor. I am going to stretch your little arm as I drag you down the hall to your bedroom. When I get to your door, I am going to kick it open, and then I am going to lift you into the air by the back of your collar and the back of your Umbro shorts. You are going to get a wedgie in your backfield as I toss you into your bed. You are then going to cry yourself to sleep. I am going to slam your door and go to bed downstairs, mad and disappointed. In the morning, I am going to wake up mad, and I am not getting in the car. I am not going to Searcy, and you are not playing in the soccer tournament, and…I am only asking…which way is it going to be? You are the boss. You are in control. We will do it either way. You choose."

Law enforcement officers have long been familiar with the phrase "We can do it the easy way or the hard way" that is at the very heart of R.E.A.C.T. (describe your audience's alternatives).

Officer: "Sir, I asked you to step out of the vehicle, and you refused. I explained why I need you to step out of the vehicle, and I asked again. Again, sir, you refused. Now, let me lay out your alternatives.

"Sir, if you do what I am asking—step back here, answer a few questions, and give me the answers I hope to hear—then you are going to get back in your vehicle, and you are going to drive down the road to your home where you will eat your food, sleep in your bed, and spend time with your wife. You will get up in the morning and go to your job.

"BUT, sir, if I do not get your cooperation, here is what will happen. It will become my job to pull you out of that vehicle and stick you handcuffed into my vehicle. You will take a ride to jail, sleep in their bed, eat their food, and tonight, sir, you just might be someone else's wife.

"Sir, you are in control of this situation, and I will proceed as you wish, AND I am only asking..."

Make your audience FEEL the need to cooperate. Emotional appeals are powerful motivators and Aristotle indicated fear is the greatest motivator. Both the fear of NOT getting something we want AND the fear of getting something we do NOT want motivates our behavior. The better you understand your audience's needs and goals, the better you can negotiate a favorable outcome.

But some people still do not cooperate. Even after asking three times, after offering your most logical reasoning and emotional appeals, some people still refuse to cooperate. So, chop their head off, right? Nope. Just one more question!

CONSULT

The next to last step is your final attempt to resolve the situation with words. By now, you should not be surprised that your final words are in the form of a question:

"Is there anything I can say to earn your cooperation?"

If they still refuse to cooperate with your request, you have come to the final step of R.E.A.C.T.

TAKE ACTION

If your audience still indicates they will not cooperate, then the time for words has come to an end, and it is time to take action. What action do you take? The very one you promised as the unattractive alternative.

I have to remind parents, teachers, and even cops to never present an option you cannot follow through on within 10 seconds. The threat can't be, "or Santa won't bring you any presents," or "I'll arrest everyone here!"

Benefits of R.E.A.C.T.

The key benefit is it works. Of course not with every audience, but everyone feels much more in control when they have a specific verbal plan. R.E.A.C.T. is easy to remember, and you feel more in control with this plan because you give up control to your audience. "You tell me; you make the choice; you are the one in control here, sir." Then when words fail and things get physical, who is to blame, the officer who presented options or "Mr. Good Citizen" who made the choice?

Thanks to videotape, essentially every traffic stop is a "public presentation." And as good as it feels to be in control of a situation with your words, it looks even better to the audiences reviewing the videotape and sitting in judgment of an officer.

Imagine a city attorney defending an officer (an officer accused of excessive force) with this videotaped confrontation: "Why did Mr. Polansky get beaten up by the officer? Let's view the videotape. Here we see the officer ask for Mr. Polansky's cooperation. Then you see Mr. Polansky refuse the officer's request to step out of the vehicle. Now we see the officer explain why he made the request, ask again, and again we see Mr. Polansky decline, this time both verbal and vulgar in his refusal to cooperate.

"You can hear the officer describe the available alternatives, and listen as the officer clearly indicates the choice is Mr. Polansky's. The citizen again refuses to cooperate. The officer asks if there is anything he could say to avoid a physical confrontation? Mr. Polansky refuses a fourth time. The officer takes hold of Mr. Polansky's arm. Then Mr. Polansky resists. Here Mr. Polansky pushes the officer, and here we see Mr. Polansky getting beaten up by the police officer. Why? Not because of the choices and decisions of the officer, but because of the choices and decisions of Mr. Polansky!"

The beautiful thing about R.E.A.C.T. is that not only is it a neat summary of several important principles of Communication Excellence (asking questions; emotional, logical, and personal appeals; and more) but R.E.A.C.T. also has practical application in our professional and private lives.

Once, while I was conducting a seminar with Arkansas police officers, one officer interrupted my lecture demanding to know, "Have you ever taught this stuff to school teachers in Riverside?" I confirmed that I had. He grumbled, "My wife has been using this stuff on me at home!" Then his expression lit up, and he proclaimed, "With pretty good success!"

Another benefit is that you can train others how to react. Trust me, my young daughter is not an idiot, and she learns fast. After just one bumpy escort upstairs and missing one soccer game, the next time she heard the words, "Let's take a look at your two alternatives here," I suddenly started getting cooperation instead of competition. Now, I may not like the attitude with which she complies, but the compliance is still voluntary!

Although a simple request will get action from my older daughter, I still have to include a logical explanation of WHY to Kendall. But rarely do I have to Take Action. Different as my daughters are, all of their teachers continue to say the same thing, "Your daughter is a very bright student and manages to get along well with everyone." I think I take more pride in the latter. I like to think maybe someone important in each of my daughter's young lives modeled communication excellence and demonstrated some universal principles of how to get what you want and still get along with others.

COPING WITH A LIAR

Everyone hates to be lied to, and I will close this chapter with a final communication plan for getting someone to tell you the truth. I referred to Jeff Winstead in earlier chapters. He was the young detective in La Marque, Texas who got a capital murder suspect to confess to the crime using a verbal plan he learned in one of my seminars. The strategy he learned in class was a simple four-step plan entitled: Coping With a Liar.

The steps to cope with a liar are embarrassingly simple. I am proud and flattered Detective Jeff Winstead used the lesson to get a very bad guy off the street.

Coping With a Liar
    Step One: Explain Your Doubts About Their Story
    Step Two: Positive Consequences of Telling the Truth
    Step Three: Negative Consequences of Telling a Lie
    Step Four: Ask For The Truth

CHAPTER TEN REVIEW:
DEVELOPING COMMUNICATION PLANS

Ten principles to guide you in life's most difficult situations:
- ❑ *Determine Your True Goal*
- ❑ *Look to the Future and Avoid the Past*
- ❑ *Choose an Appropriate Attitude to Project*
- ❑ *Start from a Position of Service*
- ❑ *Focus on the Behavior, Not the Person*
- ❑ *Acknowledge Other's Views and Feelings as Valid*
- ❑ *Anticipate Objections to Cooperate*
- ❑ *Consider Asking for the Assistance of Others*
- ❑ *Politely Ask for What You Want*
- ❑ *State Benefits of Cooperation*

A.E.I.O.U. Model of Strategic Interaction:
Step One:	*ASSUME they mean well*
Step Two:	*EXPRESS your concerns*
Step Three:	*INDICATE what you would like to have happen*
Step Four:	*OUTCOME expected*
Step Five:	*UNDERSTAND on a mutual level*

R.E.A.C.T. Model of Strategic Interaction:
Step One:	*REQUEST for cooperation*
Step Two:	*EXPLAIN why you are making the request*
Step Three:	*ALTERNATIVE choices described*
Step Four:	*CONSULT by asking if anything can be said to encourage cooperation with the request*
Step Five:	*TAKE ACTION promised*

Coping With a Liar:
Step One:	*Explain Your Doubts About Their Story*
Step Two:	*Positive Consequences of Telling the Truth*
Step Three:	*Negative Consequences of Telling a Lie*
Step Four:	*Ask For The Truth*

ELEVEN
Coping with
Chronic Complainers

The most difficult people in our lives are rarely strangers. The most difficult people are the ones we have to live and work with.

In 1981, Robert Bramson published *Coping with Difficult People*. Bramson produced the foundation of every lesson on difficult people I have encountered over the decades. The difficult personalities identified in his book have been addressed in workshops, books, and videos. They include these personalities: The Hostile-Aggressive, The Super Agreeable, The Negativist, The Silent-Unresponsive, The Know-It-All, The Complainer, and The Indecisive.

In 1994, Rick Brinkman and Rick Kirschner published *Dealing with People You Can't Stand*. Their book includes The Tank, The Yes Person, The No person, The Nothing Person, The Know-It-All, The Whiner, and The Maybe Person. They also included discussions of The Think-They-Know-It-All, The Grenade, and The Sniper to bring the total to ten personalities that are both difficult, and we hate them.

You may know several people with each difficult personality. You may know some people who have several of the difficult personalities. You may know someone who can be all of the difficult personalities on any given day.

My experience suggests, of all the difficult personalities, the one we encounter most often is The Chronic Complainer. You might refer to them as The Bitchin', Complainin' Malcontents at Work, or you may call them Whiney Cry Babies, or Victimized Drama Queens, or Grouchy Old Men.

However you refer to them, almost everyone is unfortunately all too familiar with this personality. We all know someone who spends every waking hour subjecting captive audiences to their endless criticism, condemnations, and complaints about the smallest details of their chronically miserable life.

So, let me help you find the right words to say at the right time to Your Chronic Complainer. We are going to focus on this one personality for two reasons. First, The Chronic Complainer is the most common difficult personality.   Second, the strategies for interacting with The Chronic Complainer are essentially the very same strategies and principles used to address all of the other possible difficult personalities we encounter at work and home.

UNIVERSAL PRINCIPLE OF DIFFICULT PEOPLE #1:
People Are Difficult Because It Works.

Imbedded in those six words are the secrets to understanding and strategically interacting with difficult people.

Sometimes, I am difficult. It is usually when I am not getting what I want. Sometimes, I want a little appreciation for my efforts. Usually, I want to do it my way. But sometimes, I could use a little help. I also hate to look stupid. I like to be seen as a good guy, and I expect to be paid on time. I want to be told the truth. I like to be told I am O.K., and occasionally, I just want to be left alone. I also don't like my neighbor's dog pooping in my front yard. I do not want the blame for other people's mistakes. I don't like being told what to do, and sometimes I can be a difficult person because it helps me get what I want.

Universal Principle of Difficult People #2:
*The quickest, easiest way to deal with a difficult person
is to give them what they want!*

Understanding the Chronic Complainer

"But," you may ask, "what about those who are never satisfied?" Apparently they are not ever getting what they want!

To develop a communication plan for Chronic Complainers, first you have to understand the behavior.

The key to understanding Chronic Complainers is to understand how the Four P's relate to the behavior.

The Four P's:

- ❑ Powerless
- ❑ Passive
- ❑ Prescriptive
- ❑ Perfect

You will soon see how the Four P's relate to the chronic complainer, but for now take a look at the following:

The Continuum of Self-Determination

1.................. 50 100

Low   High

Some people have this philosophy:
> *What happens to me is a result of my actions, my
> decisions, and my choices.*

Other people embrace this philosophy:
> *What happens to me is the result of luck,
> circumstance, destiny, and the actions of others.*

The people who strongly believe the self-determination described in the first philosophy would score on the High end of the scale of The Continuum of Self-Determination.

The ones who embrace the second philosophy would score on the Low end. If you absolutely buy into the idea that both constructs are equally true, give yourself a score of 50 on the continuum.

On what end of the scale do we find The Chronic Complainers? Given that their problems are never their fault, and they have extreme external explanations for all that goes wrong in their lives. The Chronic Complainers all score Low on the Continuum of Self-Determination.

Now, let's revisit The Four P's to see how they relate to an understanding of the behavior.

The Four P's:
- Powerless
- Passive
- Prescriptive
- Perfect

The Chronic Complainer is POWERLESS to do anything about the problems in their life. They are PASSIVE participants in their life affairs and PRESCRIBE blame to others for their problems. They can also PRESCRIBE to others the responsibility for solving their problems. Therefore, they see themselves as PERFECT. They believe others are the cause of their problems, and others are responsible for solving their problems.

Does this behavior work for them? You bet, because the behavior is the reward. They are free of the burden of regret because it is really not their fault things are so screwed up.

THE BEHAVIOR IS THE REWARD

The behavior is the reward because if they complain often enough, someone will speak up and give them something they want, confirmation. "You are so right; it's not your fault; it's their fault," someone in their audience agrees. Not only do they get to blame others, they have social confirmation.

WHAT IS YOUR TRUE GOAL?

With better understanding of the behavior, you are now in a better position to develop your personal communication plan. The first step to developing a communication plan (you may recall from Chapter Ten) is to determine your true goal.

"I want them to become a more optimistic person and to quit seeing the bad side of people and situations. I want them to stop criticizing, condemning, and complaining."

Dream on! Recall the first Universal Principle of Difficult People: *People are difficult because it works.*

This behavior has worked for years, sometimes decades. You can't change them with your words, so you have to change your words with them. The key to finding the right words is finding your true goal. Your problem isn't that they are complainers. Your problem is they are complaining to you. So, your goal is to stop them from complaining to you by sending them to someone else!

SWITCH TO PROBLEM SOLVING

The quickest strategy I can suggest to accomplish that goal is to switch them to solving their own problem. Do they want to take responsibility for solving their problem? NO WAY, and your problem is solved. They will go to someone else to complain, seeking someone who will agree with their worldview.

UNIVERSAL PRINCIPLE OF DIFFICULT PEOPLE #3:
Difficult behavior stops when it stops working.

The complaining behavior didn't work with you. You didn't give them sympathy, "Bless your heart, you poor, poor thing," or glorify them for suffering through such degrading victimization, "I think you are doing a great job of handling such a heavy load," or agree with their hopelessness by saying, "You are so right, there is absolutely nothing that can be done!"

With your true goal in sight, you select which attitude is best to project when interacting with Your Chronic Complainer. I suggest an attitude of Chronic Optimism to support your belief that Your Chronic Complainer can solve their own problem themselves.

BE A GOOD AUDIENCE

With your true goal, general strategy, and an appropriate attitude, you are ready to try your communication plan with Your Chronic Complainer. The next time they begin complaining to you, the hard part begins. You have to be a good audience. You have to listen very closely to their complaining. Ask for elaboration. Ask for clarification. Probe the complainer's view of the problem and their interpretations of personal accountability and responsibility for solving the problem. Listen to see if the complaining is merely cathartic, the symptom of a true crisis, or something that can be addressed by the complainer. Listen very closely for clues to how you can empower them to correct their own complaint.

Paraphrase what the complainer is saying often, "Let me make sure I understand you. What you are saying is…"

SWITCH TO PROBLEM SOLVING

Then summarize the complainers position and say, "Here is what I think you can do to begin solving your problem yourself..."

Win-Win for you. Either they take responsibility or they take their complaint to someone else. Your problem is solved! And the next time Your Chronic Complainer has a problem they expect you to solve, you optimistically suggest they can solve it themselves, again, and again.

And the behavior stops because it stops working.

THE WHINEY CRY BABY COP

For years, the material above on communicating with The Chronic Complainers was the material I shared with both university students in conflict management classes and law enforcement professionals in professional development seminars. I got the sense that Chronic Complaining was a common behavior observed in police departments. Not that anyone admitted to being a Chronic Complainer, but I sensed just about everyone in law enforcement seemed certain they worked with some at their agency.

After a lecture over the above material, my intuition was confirmed. An Arkansas law enforcement officer handed me an article on the topic of complainers that he thought I might find interesting. I did!

The article was a reprint of an article on the Medley, Florida Police Department website. Chief Patrick Kelly authored the article, *Dealing With the Whining Cry Baby*.

Chief Kelly's opening paragraph confirmed what I suspected about police departments. I also suspect many of the same complaints are heard in the halls of civilian organizations as well. His article began, "Hear it? Hear that high-pitched, annoying, constant background noise? One thing is for sure: it's getting louder and more persistent, and there is no getting away from it. If you can make out some of the words, they sound like: The department doesn't appreciate me. The department won't help me plan my career. No one ever tells me what's going on around here. The Chief is a jackass. My evaluation wasn't fair. My last raise was too long ago and too small. Everything's changing too fast and not for the better. It's not fair. This place stinks. And the granddaddy of them all, morale is lower than it's ever been. Waaaaaaaaaah…"

If the last complaint sounds familiar to you, I'm not surprised. I am occasionally asked by Police Departments to conduct Communication Assessments of the agency. The assessment is largely a 100-item survey about organizational communication and is completed by all personnel at an agency. The data analysis includes a rank ordering of the 100 items to evaluate a particular agency's strengths and weaknesses related to internal communication. No agency ever answers the 100 questions the same. Every agency's answers to the 100 questions produce a unique rank ordering except for one question.

Police departments almost always rate the same question as the lowest rated item on the 100-item survey. The one question asked which receives the absolute lowest agreement is the statement, "Attitudes towards work and morale are good in this organization."

Why? Why does it seem that we all work with so many Chronic Complainers? Why do there seem to be more and more complainers all the time?

I'll answer with a quick story.

I WANT A CANDY BAR!

I was visiting my former hometown on business and entered a local 5K race that had hundreds of runners gathering at the 8:00 am starting line. Way ahead of me on the crowded sidewalk, I spotted an old friend from high school. I had not seen Mike since we ran high school track together. I hurried past dozens of people to catch up with him. He and his wife were both fit, participating in the race, and eager to find his parents. His parents were to serve as babysitters for the couple's two daughters. His oldest was about five and was accompanied by her infant sister in a baby carriage pushed down the sidewalk by her mother. Mike introduced me to his family, and we began visiting.

Soon, our conversation was interrupted. Mike's five year-old daughter, Erika, started whining, "I want a candy bar! I WANT a candy bar! I WANT A CANDY BAR!"

It was like fingernails on a chalkboard but only to me. Her parents seemed immune to the screeching demand for satisfaction—NOW! Finally, Mike's wife said, "Hush up, Erika! We don't have any candy bars," as she turned back to our conversation. I began speaking. Again, I was interrupted by, "I WANT A CANDY BAR!"

Her mother said, "We don't have any candy bars!"

Did I mention Erika was one fat little five year-old? Oh yeah, built like the Michelin Man only a lot louder and more annoying. Talk about your cognitive dissonance. I meet two strikingly fit parents, and in the next breath, I am introduced to their especially fat kid.

I began speaking again, and this time I saw young Erika slip around her mother and over to the diaper bag on her sister's baby carriage. I saw her unzip it and peer inside. I glanced down and saw the expected diapers and wipes. I also spotted something else in that diaper bag. Care to guess?

No, I didn't see a candy bar. I saw a Sam's Club super-sized package of 40 candy bars. The package was missing the top few candy bars, and I could see Erika struggling to get her chubby fingers under the cellophane and into the package far enough to reach her goal.

Her mother saw her reaching into the bag, jerked Erika's arm out, and slapped her on the wrist admonishing her, "I said you can't have a candy bar. Now, hush up and quit interrupting. Go on Brian…"

I began, yet again, awaiting the inevitable. Moments later, my fears were confirmed when Erika pitched a full scale fit on the crowded sidewalk screaming, "I WANT MY CANDY BAR!"

Now I was anxiously on the lookout for a babysitting grandparent to take this kid away. They didn't. But guess what did make an appearance on that crowded sidewalk. You bet. Her mother reached into that bag, pulled out a candy bar, and practically shoved it down her daughter's soon contented face. I then heard, "Go on with what were you saying."

****

WHY SO MANY WHINEY CRY BABIES?

Why are there so many Chronic Complainers, and why does there seem to be more and more of them? Here is one theory:

BAD PARENTING

Dr. Charles Smith teaches parent-child relations at Kansas State University and says parents are responsible for the behavior of their children. He says, "A child whines because they have learned that kind of repetitive, aggravating behavior gets them what they want. Parents have to realize that they created this behavior, and now they're going to have to suffer through it."

We all suffer. We suffer because these kids grow up learning the behavior works. They get what they want! They grow up in environments where the behavior is modeled, rewarded, and supported by parents who are unable or unwilling to teach responsibility, accountability, and discipline to their kids.

Teachers suffer in the classroom when the student claims, "I didn't do it; everyone else is doing it; you are only picking on me because…" These kids grow up and whine their way into my college classroom demanding, "I want an 'A'! It's not fair! They got an 'A', and I want my 'A'; I am going to the Dean; I am going to complain; you are just picking on me because…"

Then, with their undeserved grade in hand, they show up at your place of employment and accept a job. And the next thing you hear is, "It's not my fault; it's their fault. I don't want to work with them any more! I want to work over there with them doing that, not here doing this with these people. I want a new vehicle; I want a new shift; I want that promotion; I am going to sue; I want freedom of information; you are just picking on me because..."

Sometimes, the easiest way of dealing with a difficult person is to just give them what they want so they will finally shut up.

My wife has long been grateful our kids don't whine. Our daughters are quick to admit they have it pretty good and will, occasionally, even admit they are grateful. My daughters have never fussed at or with each other, and their parents are both grateful. But I am taking some credit.

I am taking credit because I know me, and I know I just can't stand whining. It is on my short list of intolerable behaviors somewhere below murder and above scratching fingernails on a chalkboard. I trust my kids are both capable of perceived injustices and, as bright kids, were certainly motivated by self-interest at a young age. I trust both, on some occasion, tried the Whining Cry Baby routine on me. And I trust we had a brief, immediate conversation: "Look that tone bothers me, and you cannot use that tone with me. It drives me crazy. Young lady, you are whining in the hope that I will give you what you want. It will not work and it will not be rewarded. That whiney crybaby tone you just used is forbidden for the best reason possible. It is NOT in your best interest to whine. EVER. You ask and make a good logical argument supporting why I should comply with your request, and I'll consider it. Look, Daddy is on your side. I will always do what is in your best interest, and that whiney crybaby tone is definitely NOT. Got it? Good, now let me tell you what I am going to do for you, young lady!"

Low Self-Esteem

Low self-esteem is another possible explanation. How do you know someone is suffering from low self-esteem? One way would be to listen to them. Listening to how someone talks will give you clues as to whether they have a high or low self-esteem.

Imagine someone with a low self-esteem. Are they willing and able to give compliments to others? Are they willing to criticize other people? Can they take criticism? How about taking a compliment? Does one with high self-esteem react to criticism in the same way as his colleague suffering from low self-esteem. I think not.

People who feel O.K. truly want others to feel O.K. The opposite holds true for people who are sure they are NOT O.K.! And people with high self-esteem recognize criticism for what it is, data. The comment doesn't have to be proven false or appropriate. The criticism is good information, and the person with high self-esteem concludes, "This information should prove useful in my interactions with this poor, pitiful thing trying to drag me down."

What I Miss About University Teaching

One thing I miss about teaching young college students is the opportunity to talk about the role of self-esteem in our interactions with others and, more importantly, how we talk to ourselves. We would spend time talking about the external roles of media, peers, and parents in the development of our self-image. As a professor, I had the opportunity to discuss the possibility of talking yourself into having a higher self-esteem.

One step would be to start talking like a person with high self-esteem. Resist the chance to sound like someone who abdicates all responsibility for the events in their personal and professional life.

Embrace the terminology and language of absolute accountability associated with high self-esteem.

Can a person with low self-esteem apologize? No, because the key part of a sincere apology is an admission that "I was wrong." I strongly encouraged my students to immediately find and apologize to someone who deserves their apology. Practice the language of high self-esteem. Find at least one person and say, "What I did to you was wrong, and I apologize. I promise it won't happen again, and I will do all I can to make up for the wrong I have done to you." And I reminded them, "If you can't think of anyone who deserves your apology, then you really have got a problem."

Why so many Chronic Complainers? I will give you one more reason why, but first a short story about a young police officer in a small Arkansas town.

COMPLAINERSVILLE

Years ago, I conducted some research on eight police departments using my 100-item Communication Assessment Survey. Again, my research found that the lowest rated item for all eight of the agencies was the statement, "Morale and attitudes toward work are good in this department." However, compared to the other seven agencies, one agency had particularly harsh evaluations of their small town police department. We will call that town "Complainersville."

.Each participating department was promised a report with recommendations within two weeks of completion. Typically, I would get the surveys to an agency on Monday and pick up the completed surveys on Friday so I could get started on the report. I didn't get back to "Complainersville" on Friday, as planned, to pick up the surveys. I meant to go on Saturday but didn't. I finally got up first thing on Sunday morning and made the drive to "Complainersville." I arrived at 7:30 a.m. to find the front door of this Mayberry-like town's police station locked.

I rang the buzzer. After a few minutes, I saw a young man I didn't recognize approach the glass door. When he got to the door, the young officer demanded, "Can I help you?"

I explained that I was Dr. Brian Polansky, and I was here to pick up surveys the entire department had completed that week. I'll never forget his tone and his words, "Well, no one told me nothing about that," and he then stared me down.

I said, "Look I drove a long way to get here, and I really need the surveys back today. Please call your captain, lieutenant, sergeant, anybody in the department, mention my name, and tell them what I want."

He turned, walked away, and within 60 seconds returned to unlock the door with a brand new attitude. "Sure, Dr. Polansky. I completed that survey and can take you to them! I've heard great things about your seminars. Hope I can attend someday. I just started with the department."

He took me to an office, and I spotted the box I had left for collecting the surveys. I started to pick the box up off the floor, but the young officer insisted he carry it to my car. He escorted me to my car and politely asked that I get the door open for him to set the box in my back seat. I complied. As I opened my car door, I caught a glimpse of the officer's nametag. The name "PYLE" was engraved on the tag. I smiled all the way back to Little Rock about the gung ho and enthusiastic young cop so obviously delighted to be a law enforcement officer and to be in the service of others.

Eight months later, I was conducting a seminar for municipal police officers in Arkansas. Only a dozen were enrolled, and just as I began speaking, I saw a familiar face slip into the back row. I glanced at my roster and saw that I had a student from "Complainersville" named Pyle enrolled. Well, I said to myself, isn't this going to be nice to have young Pyle in my class for eight hours.

Within the first hour, I realized I was wrong. Having young Pyle in my class was a real pain. I couldn't ever recall having a more reluctant, sarcastic, and critical participant in a seminar. Every comment was met with a smirk or a heavy sigh accompanied by a roll of the eyes. With only a dozen participants, Pyle stuck out in the worst way.

This being early in my career, I made the mistake of giving him a voice in the seminar. "Hell, who needs words when you got a gun!" he smirked. I would suggest that Arkansas towns don't pay their cops very well and Pyle would moan, "Hell, I am probably the worst paid cop you will ever meet!" I suggested the possibility that their supervisor might be an idiot. "The only bigger idiot is his boss, the Chief," a voice boomed out from the back row.

I wondered what had happened to the helpful and enthusiastic young Pyle I met just eight months ago. What happened, I wondered?

****

CHRONIC COMPLAINING IS CONTAGIOUS

I wondered what had happened until I remembered he was from "Complainersville." Apparently, in a matter of months, young Pyle had become infected with the local malady I had noted so rampant in the surveys completed by his more experienced colleagues in "Complainersville": complaints about pay, supervisors, the mayor, the state, citizens, promotions, vehicles, holidays, radios, schedules, and more complaints than all of the other seven departments' studies combined. Trust me, you talk like the culture that you live and work in. Just eight months in "Complainersville" changed young Pyle's language, vocabulary, and worldview.

One of the biggest problems of Chronic Complainers is the damage they do to others. They infect the minds of young innocents standing nearby, newcomers looking to fit in and eager to model the behaviors of those they look up to in their new careers. The young victims serve as new audiences for the Chronic Complainers: victims who listen to litanies of self-centered justifications for apathy, rebellion, and sabotage of police initiatives and policy changes.

Consequently, we all need communication plans for coping with Chronic Complainers. I believe administrators hire me for this lecture more than any presented in all the previous chapters.

STRATEGIES FOR COMMUNICATING WITH THE CHRONIC COMPLAINER

CHRONIC OPTIMISM

First, try to counter their pessimism with a shock and awe display of optimism. My wife is a master of this strategy of deflecting anger and despair. She is great at saying, "Maybe, but I think....", "Sure, but you have to agree...", "Of course, but I have also found..." and she points out the strongest arguments in the most gentle way that the glass could also be optimistically seen as half full.

Most chronic complainers are persistent in their comfortable worldview. Recognizing that Melissa is a hopeless case, they end up doing one of two things. They make a hasty retreat and go elsewhere to find social confirmation of their victim status, or they change the topic to one they find positive and uplifting and share that with Melissa. Win-Win for my side.

CHANGE THE TOPIC FOR THEM

Melissa is also a master of the dual talent of absolutely ignoring the negative condemnation and moving on to a completely new topic that hopefully engenders some positive interaction, "I'm sorry, but did you see the news last night? Oh, there was just the sweetest story about a lost puppy!" Once again, since complaining is the reward, the complaining behavior stops when the behavior stops being rewarded.

GIVE THEM MORE THAN THEY WANT

Sympathy and glory are what complainers often want, so give it to them in abundance. "Oh bless your heart, you poor, poor thing! You really have a difficult time of things. Bless you for persevering!" Chief Kelley reports about an office manager who had just about enough of a colleague's complaints about her husband. Finally, one Monday morning the manager greeted her with, "What did the moron you are married to do this weekend?" Startled, she asked, "What are you saying about my husband?" He explained that, based on her typical Monday morning reports of her weekend, he had come to the conclusion that the man must be a sadistic monster. She responded, "He is not that bad," and the complaining stopped.

BE DIRECT

This is more my style, "Hey, stop with the complaints and negativity will you, please? Your complaining is not helping me in the least bit, and frankly it isn't in your best interest either! Might I suggest you try and actually do something to solve your problem, or at least, keep your perceived hopelessness to yourself."

ASK FOR COMPLAINTS IN WRITING

If you enjoy a position of authority over your Chronic Complainer, invite them to put the complaint in writing and offer to meet after the complaint is detailed on paper. Most recognize that a formal documentation of their petty grievance is not in their best interest and drop the issue. For the persistent complainers who do produce a written document, you meet with your final strategy in mind.

SWITCH TO PROBLEM SOLVING

After an opportunity to fully determine whether the complaint is a legitimate concern or a perceived injustice, you sit down with your complainer for a meeting. "I have read your complaint and determined that you are in a position to solve your own problem. What would you like to happen, and how are you going to handle the situation?"

What you do is start shoving your Chronic Complainer east along the Continuum of Self-Determination. That is what good leaders, managers, and parents do for their important audiences. They empower others, give them hope, and encourage personal responsibility and accountability.

FIVE CONCLUSIONS ABOUT MALCONTENT COPS

One evening, as I was doing research for my seminars, I plugged "malcontent cops" into my web search and found an article posted on the web by Gilmartin, Harris & Associates on the topic of malcontent cops. The article led me to five conclusions about malcontent cops:

1. They are a common and visible problem for their departments.
2. Today's malcontents were yesterday's shining examples and model officers.
3. They expect too much from their job.
4. Departments share in the blame.
5. Malcontents do a poor job of talking to themselves.

Every police department can identify a few malcontents within their department's ranks. Citizen complaints, wrecked vehicles, negativity, anger, and chronic complaining are but a few of the symptoms readily identified.

Experienced officers are the most likely candidates to be a department malcontent, the very officers who were at one time model officers, enthusiastic about their role and their duties. I am reminded that my biggest complaining students at the university were my graduate students, especially the second year grad students. Why? Expectations. By the time a student has reached the last semesters of their university classes, they have developed some expectations about how their work should be evaluated and exactly what is the appropriate amount of work for a university professor to assign. When they were new to the organization, as freshmen and sophomores, they had no expectations and gladly did all that was expected of them without complaint. But, as the years passed, their expectations became set. And like my young officer in "Complainersville," their youthful enthusiasm can quickly give way to cynicism and resentment.

Malcontents expect too much from the job of police officer. Upon the completion of academy training, at long last, the young recruits are sworn in as police officers. Enthusiastic, they jump into their new duties with the expectation that they will now finally be happy. With a new identity, a new job, a steady paycheck, and the opportunity to make important differences, they expect to be happy being a cop. Security needs satisfied, self-esteem needs, social needs, approval needs, and self-actualization needs all finally satisfied by their new job.

After a few years, their expectations are violated. The officer now concludes, "I am not happy; I don't feel secure; my financial needs aren't being met; my needs for inclusion and approval have been repeatedly violated; my choices are limited; it is hopeless; it is out of my control; now I am angry and depressed!" And whose fault is it? There must be some external explanation for their unhappiness. The malcontents conclude, "It must be my employer, this no good police department that is taking advantage of me and my good efforts. It is their fault I am so unhappy!"

Departments do share in the blame. Inconsistent policies, unmet promises, highly directive management, and offering little appreciation for heroic efforts will lead to an agency having more than the expected occasional disgruntled employee.

In my research and work with this organizational problem, one conclusion is clear: Malcontents do a consistently poor job of talking to everyone, but the one person they do the worst job of talking to is himself or herself.

FIVE BIGGEST COMPLAINTS ABOUT BEING A COP

When I do seminars with cops, I ask them, "What are the five biggest complaints cops make about being a cop?" Audiences consistently identify the same five complaints as most common:
1. Pay
2. Schedules and hours
3. Politics and policies
4. Public support and recognition
5. Equipment

I am not a cop, never been a cop, and never wanted to be a cop. As an outsider looking in at that list of five complaints, I don't get it. I don't see why any police officer would complain about any of those five items. I conclude this lecture to officers by asking these five questions:
1. Did someone lead you to believe that government work in general, and police work in particular, is a great place to find financial security?
2. Did you think that accepting a paycheck at a 24-hour social service organization would somehow be inconvenient to only your colleagues' preferred schedules?
3. Did you think that work in municipal government would be free of politics?

4. Did you really expect the public to give you all the recognition you think is appropriate?
5. Did you think that the city budget is open to the police department to spend money on all the equipment you think is needed?

I'll close this chapter the same way I close this lecture. If you answered "Yes" to any of the five questions above and you spend any amount of time complaining about any of the five most common complaints heard in both government and civilian organizations, then let me offer you this:

Lord, grant you the courage to change the things you can,
The serenity to accept the things you cannot change,
And the wisdom to know the difference.

The five biggest complaints about being a cop are made in all police departments and civilian organizations. If you aren't happy being a cop or working your job, well then, exactly whose fault is that? The biggest lies we tell are the lies we tell ourselves. Three of the most common "useful lies" we tell ourselves:

It is hopeless,
It is not my fault,
And there is nothing I can do about it!

CHAPTER ELEVEN REVIEW:
COPING WITH CHRONIC COMPLAINERS

Three Universal Principles of Difficult People:
- ❏ *People are difficult because it works!*
- ❏ *The quickest, easiest way to deal with difficult people is to give them what they want.*
- ❏ *Difficult behavior stops when it stops working.*

The true goal is not to change the complainer but rather to change their audience to someone other than you.

Switch chronic complainers to solving their own problems, and your problems are solved.

Five Reasons There Seem to be More Chronic Complainers:
- ❏ *Bad parenting*
- ❏ *The behavior is rewarded*
- ❏ *Low self-esteem*
- ❏ *Little personal accountability*
- ❏ *The behavior is contagious in workplaces*

Six Strategies for Coping with Chronic Complainers:
- ❏ *Chronic optimism*
- ❏ *Change the topic for them*
- ❏ *Give them more than they want*
- ❏ *Be direct*
- ❏ *Ask for details in writing*
- ❏ *Switch to problem solving*

Some find peace in accepting they cannot change some things and focus their energies on the things they can.

If you hate your job, whose fault is that?

TWELVE
Your Most
Valuable Verbal Skill

In most of the previous chapters, I have argued that asking questions is your most important verbal skill. You may have said to yourself, "I get it, ASK. But sometimes you just have to tell other people something." You are correct! There are times when you just have to tell them something. How else would they know if you don't tell them?

Let me suggest when you feel compelled to tell them a thing or two that you use your most valuable verbal skill. You tell them the one thing they want to hear more than anything else, AND it is the one thing they can't ask for—your praise! I suggest that you tell them they are O.K.!

If you want to immediately begin to apply the single most valuable words the important people in your life want to hear from you, here are a final handful of tips on how to give people what they want to hear the most.

PUT IT IN WRITING

I became convinced that Giving Praise is our most valuable verbal skill after I read in Jerry Twentier's book, *The Positive Power of Praising People,* about the winner of an 111 million dollar Wisconsin Lottery. When asked by the media what he planned to do now that he and his fiancé had just won 111 million dollars, he indicated he was going back to his job as a high school English teacher.

"Why?" the collected press wanted to know.

"Because there is something in that high school that is more valuable to me than 111 million dollars," the new multi-millionaire explained. "You see, in that school is my classroom, and in my classroom is my desk. In my desk is a drawer, and in that drawer is a folder. And in that folder is every letter and every note of appreciation I have ever received from a student telling me that I was an important person, someone who made an important difference in that student's life. I believe my Lord put me on this Earth for me to make important differences. While I will make important differences with my money, I plan to continue to make the most important differences I can through my efforts in that classroom."

You may be like that guy. I am. I keep every note from every student and seminar participant who has ever taken the time to write and say, "Thank you. You helped me."

RARE WORDS ARE VALUABLE WORDS

Once, I was seated in the training secretary's office in a large Texas police department. I was waiting for copies to be made of a handout I was to use in a seminar that day. As I sat waiting, my eyes scanned all the personal items in her office. I quickly determined that her two passions were her two sons and the Dallas Cowboys. All of the decorations and personal items on her desk, shelves, walls, and bulletin board were either photos of her active sons or Dallas Cowboy memorabilia.

I noticed tacked onto a cork bulletin board was a small card with the words "Thank You" embossed on the outside. Curious, I opened the card to reveal the handwritten words, "Thank you for being such a terrific secretary to me and the department."

When she returned, I asked her why she kept that card on her bulletin board? She said, "Because it is so rare!"

****

I encourage you to not make your kind words of recognition, appreciation, and encouragement rare words. Words of praise are valuable even when freely distributed.

Look Hard for the Good and Praise It

I ask my participants to identify the one person in their life who is the most difficult to praise. I then remind them they have just identified the one person in their life who needs their praise more than anyone else. If someone like me who is pretty sure he is O.K. is still hungry for applause at the end of the day, imagine how hungry those who never get ANY praise are for just a little applause.

Alex Haley, the author of *Roots*, is buried in his family cemetery in Tennessee not far from where he first heard the stories of Kunta Kenta, Chicken George, and all the others from his family's life in this country. *Roots* told about how generation after generation of Alex Haley's family was subjected to the most vicious and inhuman behavior possible: families separated in the commerce of humans, abductions, slavery, tortures, mutilations, injustice, rape, and murder. Alex Haley's book and words spoke directly to the inhumanity of slavery and the continuing effects of the institution on all American families.

Alex Haley's final words are carved on his gravestone. His final resting spot is a challenge to find because he has a flat stone laid flat on his gravesite. Alex Haley's final words could have, once again, spoken directly to the continuing wounds of racial injustice. Yet his final words are these:

"Find the Good and Praise It."

Repeat Praise Overheard

If you find it difficult to create your own praise, use someone else's words. If you hear someone say something nice about someone in your life, you have a choice. You can let the words die right there, or you can ensure that the right person hears someone else's words of praise, commendation, and applause.

I HEARD IT THROUGH THE GRAPEVINE

While completing a long contract with a large police department in South Louisiana, I had gotten to know and respect my training department liaison, Sgt. Irv. The officer was not only a marathoner but also a tri-athlete and weight room junkie. As the training department's lead officer, Sgt. Irv also served as organizer of the department's Annual Fittest of the

Fit Competition between all of the department's officers. Sgt. Irv quickly informed me he was 51 years old and had won the Fittest of the Fit Competition over the department's 200 younger officers for the past two years. It didn't surprise me to look at him. Tall and muscularly built, I had a hard time accepting that he was over 40, but I didn't doubt he could win a fitness competition.

Over the previous weeks with his department's officers, I would occasionally mention Sgt. Irv. Almost immediately, one of the officers in my audience would spit his name back at me and snarl, "Sgt. Irv!"

When I asked what their problem was with Sgt Irv, someone would explain, "Sgt. Irv is so full of himself, never been a mirror that he can't stop at and look at himself in!"

Another young officer would pipe in with, "If I worked all day in a gym, I could be the Fittest of the Fit too even if I was 61 years old."

I learned that, as training officer, it was Sgt. Irv's job to get the other 200 officers in shape. Some of the department's officers apparently resented Sgt. Irv's encouragement toward physical fitness. It was also clear a number of the 20 and 30-something aged officers also resented getting their young butts beaten by a 51 year-old man in the annual fitness competition.

One day, Sgt. Irv took me to lunch. During our drive to get a couple of fitness smoothies, he pointed out a building and noted that one of the officers in my class almost ended his career at that building. Sgt. Irv told of how that officer had a drug bust staked out on the roof of that building. Something went wrong, and the officer leaped off of the roof thinking he would land on grass. Instead, he landed in the middle of a concrete staircase. The fall shattered both of his heels and lower legs. Sgt. Irv spoke with admiration for the young officer who had the chance to claim a career ending disability check but, instead, bravely forced himself through a long and torturous recovery to the point that he is back on duty and sitting in your class today.

A few minutes later, sitting at a stoplight, Sgt. Irv told me yet another officer in that class was almost killed at this exact spot when, years before, a drunk driver sped through this intersection's red light and slammed directly into the driver's side door of that officer's police cruiser. Sgt. Irv described the wreckage and the injuries to the entire left side of the officer. He spoke in detail of the prolonged efforts to remove the officer from the tangled wreckage that killed the drunk driver. As an officer on the scene, Sgt. Irv indicated he was sure that would be the last time he saw his young colleague in uniform.

Sgt. Irv then related that not only did the officer recover from his injuries, but he had also recently been awarded a promotion to detective that the Sgt. felt was both deserved and overdue.

After lunch, I returned to the classroom and began the afternoon lecture by mentioning I had gone out to lunch with Sgt. Irv. Immediately, an officer in my audience rolled his eyes and groaned, "Sgt. Irv, Mr. Arrogant!"

I said, "Hey now, Sgt. Irv said something really nice about you today."

The young officer countered, "No way in hell did he say anything nice about me!"

I asked, "Well then, how do I know that you had a chance to claim disability but chose not to? How do I know that you jumped off a building during a drug bust gone bad and shattered your heels and lower legs, and how do I know that Sgt. Irv is obviously very proud of your efforts to rehabilitate your injuries, not take the easy way out, and return to the police force?"

The entire room went quiet for a few moments. Then a voice in the back said, "Well, that was the first time Sgt. Irv has ever said anything nice about anyone in this room!"

I turned and said, "Well detective, then how do I know about your wreck with a drunk driver at the intersection of Veterans Boulevard and Williams Avenue? How do I know that the entire left side your body was broken by the driver killed in the accident, and how do I know that Sgt. Irv is certain your recent promotion to detective is both deserved and overdue?"

In the moments of stunned silence in that room, I came to realize that maybe Sgt. Irv is only complimenting his colleagues behind their back to others. I was delighted to take advantage of someone else's kind words and make sure that those who truly needed to hear them heard the words of recognition and appreciation.

****

Wait a minute! You might be saying to yourself, "Yeah right, but I am not going to rush out and start constantly telling people, 'You are O.K., and you are O.K.!' I am not going to do it because it isn't going to sound sincere."

I agree. Do not march around saying, "You are O.K.!" I want you to march over to the important people in your life and say, "You are O.K. BECAUSE…"

BE SPECIFIC

The reason my class was stunned into silence by my reciting Sgt. Irv's praise of those two officers was that the praise was so specific it was undeniable. Praise that isn't supported by specific evidence is indeed weak praise that sounds insincere, so do not do it. Always support your praise with specific reasons.

Just as riding a bike was awkward and embarrassing at first, you finally got used to it and now ride with ease and confidence. The same is true of Giving Praise with specifics.

CARE ENOUGH TO SEND THE VERY BEST?

There are actually hundreds of greeting card companies in the United States. All of these companies are competing in a multi-billion dollar business for your greeting card dollars. Why does this country need hundreds of greeting card companies employing writers, publishers, and distributors of paper with kind words on them? Why? Because we aren't very good at writing kind words to others all by ourselves!

So, every time we need some kind words, we jump in the car, drive down to the Wal-Mart, find the card section, and begin eliminating cards for our purchase. We look and look until we find the card with the right words. One company distinguishes itself from the hundreds of others by using the slogan, "When you care enough to send the very best." So, we check the back of our card to see exactly which company produced the words we want read by the important person in our life. We pick the card with words written by someone who has never seen nor will ever see the one who will receive those words we want to be read.

Look, if you truly care to send the very best, send your own words, written by your hand, and on paper that will be cherished by that important person in your life. I am also willing to bet that your words on paper will soon become one of the most valuable things that your important person will save—in a folder, in a drawer, in a desk, in the room where they keep all of their most valuable papers.

I used to keep a praise "cheat sheet" handy so if I ever struggled to find the right words to offer a word of praise, I could reach for my "cheat sheet" of praise. When I was talking on the phone or writing a note to an important person in my life, I could use my "cheat sheet" of praise to quickly find the right words to say at the right time. Below are my 20 ways to craft your praise cheat sheet. You say their name and find the most appropriate praise to specifically support your praise.

20 WAYS TO PRAISE CHEAT SHEET

I appreciate your help with…

I'm really impressed with your…

That is quite an accomplishment the way you…

You make important contributions by…

One of the things I enjoy about you is…

People admire you for…

You can be proud of yourself for…

You did an outstanding job of …

You made my day because…

You have a special talent for…

I enjoy working with you because…

It took a lot of courage when you…

No one's ever done a better job of …

You have a special gift for…

You really helped me when you…

You are fun to work with because…

I'm glad you're on my team because…

You know, you are famous for…

I appreciate how you always…

I want to thank you because…

Prepare to be Praised

The above is my final warning to anyone who begins a renewed effort to offer kind words of encouragement and support to the important people in their life. Prepare to be praised because communication is reciprocal. People do talk to others the way they are being talked to. If you are not getting enough praise and recognition in your ears, take an inventory of how much praise is coming out of your mouth!

I truly hope that my words have encouraged you to embrace a new determination to ensure that your future interactions with the most important people in your life will include the words they most want to hear from you and cannot ask you to say.

I am asking on behalf of the important people in your life. Take out a blank sheet of paper, put a pen in your hand, and begin writing. Write the next set of words that will remind one of the most important people in your life exactly why they are so important to you. Avoid the burden of regret that comes from wishing you had said something. Write the words you have been meaning to say for so long. Write the right words, right now. Put them on paper before it is too late.

CHAPTER TWELVE REVIEW:
YOUR MOST VALUABLE VERBAL SKILL

Your most valuable verbal skill is Giving Praise.

Put your praise in writing, and they will
  cherish your words forever.

Look hard for the good and praise it because the ones
  who are rarely praised are the ones who need it the most.

Repeat praise overheard, and make certain that the ones who
  need to hear the words of praise actually do hear the words.

Be very specific with your praise, and
  support your praise with specific evidence.

If you don't have enough praise coming into your ears,
  check how much praise is coming out of your mouth.

People talk to people the way they are being talked to.

Praise others and prepare to be praised by others.

Everyone wants to hear that they are O.K.!

Write the right words, right now to avoid the burden of
  regret that comes from failing to do so before it is too late.

INDEX

A.E.I.O.U. Model, 191-92
Accommodation, 137-38
Advanced Management Journal, 29
Air Force Academy, 171-72
Al Qaida, 162
Apology, 34, 59, 130, 180, 217
Appreciation, 58, 60, 97
    Notes of, 2, 230, 233
    Showing, 29-30
    and Complainers, 85-86
Argumentation, 108-09
Aristotelian Rhetorical Appeal, 150, 153, 193
Aristotle, 52, 148, 195-98
    Rhetorica, 145-47, 150
Art of conversation, 63-73
Art of competition, 137
Art of taking an order, 169
Asking questions, 44, 58-60, 127, 129
    in developing verbal plans, 188, 200
    journalistic Tools, 46
    Socratic Method, 157

Attributions, 104-05, 112
Audience identification, 52
Austin, Texas, 26
Avoidance, 106, 108, 139
Axioms, 129

Balance Theory, 110, 167
Bartlesville, Oklahoma, 138
Baton Rogue, Louisiana, 85
Bias in attributions, 104
Bramson, Robert 205
Brinkman, Rick, 205
Buddism, 21
Burden of expectations, 7, 48

Carnegie, Dale, 31-32, 51, 145-46
Change, 5, 13, 22, 107-11
Chronic complainers, 86, 205-20,
Cicero, 86
Cognitive Dissonance, 91, 96-98, 102, 106-11, 160
Communicating with Difficult People (Seminar) 4, 244-45
Communication Excellence for Medical Professionals (Seminar), 4,
Communication plans, 179-81, 184, 194, 220
Complainers, 31, 205,
    Causes and explanations, 207-09, 212, 214
    Citizen Complaints, 2, 251
    Coping with, 220-21
    in Police Departments 86, 211-12

Malcontents,   31
and Self perception, 31
Complainersville, 217-19
Conflict, 95, 120, 124, 126
    Axioms of Conflict, 129-30
    Conflict Goals, 131-135
    Definition, 116
    and Fight or Flight, 122-126
Conflict management, 129, 134,
    139, 161
Conflict Management &
    Negotiation (Seminar), 4
Conflict Outcomes, 136-141
Confucianism, 21
Continuum of Self-
    Determination, 207-08, 222
Conversations, 41, 64, 84, 106,
    189
    DERA Structure in, 82-84
    Helping conversations, 78-83
    Master the art of, 65-72
    Most important, 57
Coping with Difficult People
    (Bramson), 205
Coping with Speech Anxiety,
    123
Counseling, 75, 82, 88
Counseling psychologists, 75,
    78, 82, 111, 184
Cozumel, Mexico, 10
Credibility, 52, 149, 150
Chronemics, 39

Dallas Cowboys, 230
Dealing with People You Can't
    Stand (Brinkman &
    Kirschner), 205
Dealing With the Whining Cry
    Baby (Kelly), 211
Defensiveness, 50
Delaware Tribe of Indians, 138-
    39
DERA Structure, 82
DFW Airport, 187

Edison, Thomas A., 58
Emotional appeals, 148-49, 198
Empathy, 75-78, 81, 83
Enhancing Client Relations for
    Certified Public Accountants
    (Seminar), 4
Ethos, 52, 147, 149-50
Eubanks, Ralph, Ph.D., 40
External Attributions, 105

F.B.I. National Academy, 256
Facial expression, 39
Fear of getting something you
    do not want, 148, 199
Fear of looking stupid, 27-28,
    65, 122
Fear of not getting what you
    want, 148, 199
Fear of speaking in public, 27
Festinger, Leon, 97
Fight or Flight, 120-26,193
Five Step Proper Introduction,
    72
Fort Worth, Texas, 172, 183,
    187
Fundamental perceptual error,
    91, 102, 160

Gang Banging in Little Rock
    (Television), 174
Gestures, 39
Gilmartin, Harris & Associates,
    222
Golden Rule, 20, 24
Gnadenhuetten Massacre, 139-
    40

Haley, Alex 231
Hall, Wally, 91
Handshakes, 69-70
Harvey (Film), 83-84, 87
Hindu, 20

How to Win Friends & Influence People (Carnegie), 31-32, 145-46

Identity Goals, 135
Idiot's Philosophy of Human Interaction, 20
Idiots, 15, 25, 110, 174, 197
Internal Attributions, 104
International Association of Chiefs of Police, 256
Interpersonal Needs Theory, 167
Islamic, 21
It's a Wonderful Life (Film), 83

Jeopardy (Television) 27, 44
Jesus, 101, 150

Kansas State University, 214
Kelley, Jeff A., 183-85
Kelly, Patrick, 211
Kenner, Louisiana, 80
Kentucky, 32
Kinesics, 39
Kiowa, 11
Kirschner, Rick, 205

La Marque, Texas, 2, 200
Law Enforcement Management Institute of Texas, 256
Leadership & Communication Excellence (Seminar), 3, 244
Levine, Mark, 179
LifeScripts (Pollan), 179-80, 188
Lincoln, Abraham 31-35, 140, 146-49
Lincoln, Mary Todd, 33
Listening, 39, 42, 44, 81, 216
Little Rock, Arkansas, 132, 187, 218
Logos, 147-48, 160

Magic five-word question, 56
Manic-depressive, 34
Maslow, Abraham, 162
Maslow's Hierarchy of Needs, 162-66
Master Conversationalists, 64-65
McClellan, George 34
Mississippi River, 80

Native Americans, 138-39
Negotiation, 179-80, 198
New Jersey, 138
Nonverbal communication, 39, 42, 69
North Little Rock Police Department, 175, 182

One question everyone wants answered, 56
Optimism, 210, 220, 211

Paraphrasing, 79, 81
Pathos, 147-48, 160-62, 197
Penn, William, 138
Pennsylvania, 138, 140
Perceived injustices, 86, 130, 215
Personal Appeal, 154, 200
Persuasion, 42, 54, 109 145
Persuasive Skills & Professional Success (Seminar), 3, 244
Philosophy of human interaction, 19-22, 36
Platinum Rule, 22
Plato, 146-47
Pollan, Stephen 179
Positive Power of Praising People, The (Twentier), 229
Praise, 29-30, 229-36
Preview, 55
Principle of Verbal Reciprocity, 20, 82
Professional image, 16
Provisionalism, 92

Psychological Emergencies, 119
Public speaking,
    Audience reactions, 4
    Developing confidence in,
    122-3 Evaluation of, 51-52,
    55
    Fear of, 27-28, 121

Ranger Boats, 133
Rationalization, 48, 50, 107-111
R.E.A.C.T. Model, 193-200
Reciprocity, 20, 22, 82, 128
Relationship goals, 134-35
Relationships, 27, 60, 137, 156,
    203
    Difficult, 125, 142
    Intimate, 134, 139
    Most imortant, 14, 17
    Professional, 137
Remembering names, 66
Rhetoric, 127, 146-47
Rhetorica (Aristotle), 145-46,
    150
Roots (Haley), 231

San Antonio, 132
Schutz, William B., 167-75
Searcy, Arkansas, 196
Security needs, 163, 223
Self-actualization, 165, 223
Self-esteem, 148, 164, 216-17,
Self-serving attributions, 112
Smith, Charles, 214
Social Needs, 164, 223
Social Retard, 64
Socrates, 146-47, 150
South Carolina Sheriff's
    Association, 94
Springfield, Illinois, 32
Springfield, Missouri, 87
Stage fright, 122-23
Stewart, Jimmy , 83-84
Stupid people, 25

Sympathy, 75-77, 83-86, 210,
    221

Team Leadership & Coaching,
    (Seminar), 4, 244
Texas Christian University, 172
Texas Tech University Police
    Department, 30
The New Yorker , 95
Traffic Stops, 53-55, 195, 199
Traffic tickets, 189
Twentier, Jerry, 229

Uncertainty Reduction Theory,
    159-162
Universal truths, 3-4, 8, 17
University of Kansas, 1, 4, 7,
    179, 245
University of Oklahoma, 11
Unknown Lincoln, The
    (Carnegie), 31

Verbal abuse, 125
Verbal Fitness for Patrol
    Officers, (Seminar), 4
Villa, The 115-19, 121,126, 192-
    93

Wal-Mart, 117-18, 234
Washington, George 139
Wilkins, Uncle Bob, 69-70, 77,
    181
Winstead, Jeff, 2, 200-01
Win-win outcomes, 136, 140
Work stress, 16
World Trade Center, 87

Your Most Important Verbal
    Skill, 39, 43-46, 58-60, 77
    in empathy, 77
    in Active Listening, 58
    in Verbal Plans, 188, 194

Polansky Seminars

Let Dr. Brian Polansky design and present a customized educational program for your organization or association.

Titles for keynotes, workshops, and seminars include:
Persuasive Skills & Professional Success
Leadership & Communication Excellence
Communication Excellence in Customer Service
Advanced Verbal Fitness for Enhanced Professionalism
Communicating with Difficult People
Team Leadership & Coaching
Ethics & Excellence

Specialized programs are available for professionals in
Financial Services
Judicial Education
Health Care and Medicine
Education
Law Enforcement
Corporate Security
Government Service and Administration

For more information contact:

Polansky & Associates
501-221-1976
brianpolansky@msn.com

About the Author

Dr. Brian Polansky is Law Enforcement's Communication Professor, and an award-winning educator, speaker, author, and developer of education programs designed to encourage professional success through communication excellence.

After completing a Doctorate in Communication Studies at the University Of Kansas, Dr. Polansky joined the faculty of the University of Arkansas-Little Rock as a professor. He has provided communication education and curriculum development to law enforcement agencies including the F.B.I. National Academy, the U.S. Attorney's Office, Law Enforcement Management Institute of Texas, International Association of Police Chiefs, and police academies and leadership schools throughout the United States.

Dr. Polansky is now president of Polansky & Associates and presents continuing education seminars to a wide variety of professionals in corporate business, finance, health care, education, corporate security, and government service. Popular seminar topics include *Communication Excellence, Persuasive Skills, Verbal Fitness, Team Leadership* and *Communicating with Difficult People*.

Visit **www.brianpolansky.com** to learn more about how to schedule a workshop, seminar, or keynote presentation for your organization or call 501-221-1976.

To order additional book copies and information about new titles visit **www.ArrowRidgePublishing.com**.